TRIAL BY AMBUSH

Federal Agent Turned Rat

DESTRY JARRETT

This is a book of fiction. Names, characters, places and incidents are the product of the author's imagination or used fictitiously and any resemblance to actual persons, living or dead, business or companies, events or local is entirely coincidental

DIOV Publishing Group

P.O. Box 980136

Houston, Texas 77098

DIOV Publishing Group is a division of V12EXOTICS LLC

WWW.DIOVBOOKS.COM

Library of congress cataloging-in-publication data

ISBN (978-0-578-39278-3)

Printed USA

DEDICATION

We would like to thank the following for giving us permission to use their work:

TONY SERRA- Civil Rights attorney and activist

F.LEE BAILEY-Former criminal defense attorney, author actor and businessman.

Sidney Powell-Federal appellate attorney and author of "Licensed To Lie" and Co-Author of "Conviction Machine"

Harvey Silverglate-Co-Author of "Conviction Machine",

MARTIN YANT- Private investigator and author, lead private investigator at Ace investigations. An investigation Martin launched while editor of the Mansfield, Ohio, News Journal led to the conviction of the county sheriff and seven deputies.

SCOTT BULLOCK- is an American lawyer who focuses on property rights issues such as eminent domain and civil forfeiture.

H.MICHAEL STEINBERG- Colorado criminal lawyer specializing in Colorado criminal law for 35 years.

PAMELA COLLOFF- Is American journalist who has written for The New Yorker and Texas Monthly where she was an executive editor.

ERIC UMANSKY- Deputy managing editor of ProPublica where he has overseen two Pulitzer Prize winning projects

PROLOGUE

The Union of the South (U.S.) is a sprawling country in South America. Among its territories, Americana stands as the largest and most influential state. Deep within the capital, the federal government covertly intercepts the phone conversations of thousands of its own citizens every single day. Operating through a vast network of illegal wiretaps, a faction of corrupt federal agents uses sophisticated software to spy on the nation's most powerful figures—listening in on politicians, defense attorneys, and elected officials to control the country from the shadows.

TRIAL BY AMBUSH

Federal Agent Turned Rat

DIOV PUBLISHING GROUP

TABLE OF CONTENTS

CHAPTER ONE

The FBS and the whole Department of Justice have a number of tools that are calculated that can get anyone prosecuted or credibly threatened with prosecution. Once they do that, it's easy to turn any average person, any law-abiding person into an informant.

Inside the stark, windowless room of the federal facility, the air-conditioning hummed a low, aggressive tune. Two investigators sat across a metal table from the former field operative.

The lead investigator slid a stack of official forms across the scratched steel.

"Agent Hammon, can you sign these forms agreeing to this debriefing?"

"Yes," Hammon replied. He picked up the pen and signed his name with a steady hand.

The investigator leaned forward, clicking the record button on the digital device between them. "Tell us about your training as an undercover agent."

"I trained for three years before going into the field," Hammon said, staring directly into the lens of the recording camera. "It was called corruption school."

The second investigator frowned, looking up from his legal pad. "Why was it called corruption school?"

"Because," Hammon said softly, "they taught us to flip anything a suspect told us into a crime"

The lead investigator flipped to the next page of the transcript, his eyes scanning the logged phone numbers.

"How is he in this investigation?" the lead investigator asked.

"He was one of the phone contacts," Hammon explained, leaning back in his chair. "This is a guy who did drugs, and turned his life around and we listened to his phone conversations for years."

The investigator tapped the file. "Why target him if he was clean?"

Hammon didn't hesitate. "Look, this is John! He works two jobs, has millions of subscribers on social media, and makes thousands of dollars playing video games online. We have no reason to listen to his calls, but we did."

The second investigator looked up, his pen pausing over the paper. "Is there a culture of corruption?"

"Yes," Hammon said bluntly. He reached across the table, pulling another profile from the stack. "Here is another guy named Charles. He owns a real estate inspection business. Why are we looking into him?"

"Were any of these individuals committing crimes?" the lead investigator asked.

"No," Hammon replied.

"Is there corruption in the internet tracking team?"

"Yes."

"What is it?"

Hammon leaned completely across the tsable, his voice dropping to a dangerous register. "They are doing surveillance using smart internet wireless devices."

The room went dead silent. The lead investigator blinked, trying to process the statement. "What does that mean?"

"They can listen to your conversation at your house, if the refrigerator is hooked up to the wifi," Hammon said.

The lead investigator crossed his arms, staring hard at the former agent. "How does it work?

The lead investigator leaned forward, his elbows resting heavily on the cold metal table. He stared at Hammon, trying to fully comprehend the scale of what the former agent was describing.

"How does it work?" the lead investigator asked.

"They can turn on any electric device that is connected to wifi in your house and turn it into a listening device," Hammon said flatly.

He didn't blink. He said it with the casual detachment of a man explaining how a light switch works.

"If it has a microchip and an antenna, it belongs to the team."

The second investigator looked up from his legal pad, adjusting his glasses.

"We want to shift the direction of the questionings, give us the capabilities of the IMSI catchers."

Hammon nodded slowly. "We can look at suspects' call logs, text messages, and even listen to their phone calls in real time. The IMSI catcher mimics a cell tower. The suspect's phone connects to it automatically, thinking it's a secure network.

Once they bypass that gate, the target's entire digital life is laid bare. Nothing is hidden."

"Did you employ neighbors of the suspects?" the lead investigator asked.

"Yes," Hammon said, his voice dropping into a deeper, darker register. "We used any contact with the suspect to turn on them, even family members. We would find a vulnerability—an unpaid tax bill, an old arrest, a secret—and we would squeeze them

until they agreed to spy on the person living next door or sleeping across the hall."

The room grew quiet for a moment, the heavy hum of the building's ventilation system filling the silence. The second investigator flipped his page, his eyes locking onto a sensitive section of the debriefing outline.

"Did you ever keep any of the money you stole from suspects?"

"Yes," Hammon admitted without a shred of hesitation.

"Did you turn any of it in?" the lead investigator followed up.

"Yes."

"Did you keep any drugs?" the second investigator asked.

"Yes."

The lead investigator leaned closer, his eyes narrowing. "What did you do with the drugs?"

"I gave it to family members, other agents, and cops who had contacts that could sell it," Hammon said. The revelation hung in the air like a thick fog.

The very people tasked with cleaning the streets of Americana were operating as the primary distributors, utilizing a closed loop of seized contraband to fund their own black-market networks.

The lead investigator swapped a long, calculating look with his partner. He tapped his fingers on the recording device, evaluating the sheer weight of Hammon's confession.

"Can we get you to wear a wire to corroborate what you're saying?"

Hammon smiled, a cold, humorless expression. "Sure."

Hammon leaned back in his steel chair, looking up at the ceiling lights. The reality of the law enforcement landscape in Americana was far more complex than a few rogue operatives stealing cash and wiretapping refrigerators.

"The number one civil rights attorney in the country is airing commercials, telling our citizens to call him if you feel your rights have been violated," Hammon murmured, almost to himself. "He knows what's happening out there. He tells them: *'Do not talk to the FBS without your attorney present. Any false statement to anyone in the federal government can get you indicted.'*"

The second investigator sighed, tapping his pen.

"He's right. The system is rigged to turn a conversation into a felony."

"Exactly," Hammon agreed. "Good cops are being put in the same basket as dirty cops, who rob, frame, and kill with no consequences. The good ones get squeezed out or forced into silence by the culture. Look at the internal dynamics alone. Female cops are in a male-dominated environment, where their male superiors decide on their promotions. If they don't play along, their careers are dead. The unwritten rule is absolute: back your brother and sister in blue, even if they are violating the law."

"And what about the informants?" the lead investigator asked.

"Snitches are a way of life for law enforcement," Hammon said, shaking his head. "They drive them around pointing out suspected criminals, and they search these same suspects without a warrant. It's an ambush from start to finish. There's an old adage in the prosecution world, it's easy to indict a ham sandwich if the grand jury only hears one side. But out on the streets, the ambush is even easier."

The lead investigator turned his attention back to the primary log book on the metal desk.

He adjusted the microphone of the recording device, wanting to establish a clear, unassailable baseline for the official record on the specific targets they had bypassed regular warrants to track.

The lead investigator checked the next block of questions on his debriefing sheet.

"We want to shift the direction of the questioning, give us the capabilities of the IMSI catchers."

Hammon closed his eyes, the sheer volume of intercepted data rushing back into his mind. "I know humans' secrets. I listened to calls all day long, for thirty years."

The lead investigator remained silent, letting the tape roll.

"I know where senators eat lunch, governors vacation for winter, and presidents hide their mistresses," Hammon said, his voice dropping to a gravelly whisper.

"You can't move in Union South

without being recorded. Every digital footprint is saved, logged, and categorized. I fight for the underdog—drug dealers, bank robbers, and cartel members—because they are the only ones who actually know they are at war with the state."

He opened his eyes, staring directly at the investigators.

"The war on drugs is where they get their promotions. They lie and cheat to move up the ladder. Every major bust is stepping stone built on manufactured evidence and broken laws."

The scene shifts from the interrogation room to the brutal reality of the legal aftermath.

Life without parole is what happens when an ex-cop decides to go to trial. Your back is against the wall before the trial even starts. The prosecutors come at you with a mountain of intercepted data, twisted statements from your time in 'corruption school,' and a jury pool that has already been poisoned by the media.

"Raise your right hand," the bailiff's voice echoed in Hammon's memory.

"Should I take the stand?"

"Who can I trust?"

These are some of the questions I asked myself for years, and if I had to do it all over again, I would.

"Why? I keep asking myself," Hammon reflected, his mind tracing the long, cold layout of his current reality. "How could I be found guilty for a crime I didn't commit?"

Once you've spent years in solitary confinement, you're able to see more clearly. The noise of the world fades away, replaced by the stark, unyielding truth of your choices. Doing the right thing comes with consequences.

The tape recorder continued to spin, its internal gears clicking softly in the small interrogation room. The lead investigator shifted the weight of his body against the back of his chair, reviewing the massive, repeating patterns in the wiretap database log.

"Let's review the parameters of the digital collection cycle once more," the lead investigator said, his voice flat

Hammon did not flinch. He looked at the paperwork, then back at the lens of the recording camera. "How is he in this investigation?"

The lead investigator pointed to the secondary profile sheet attached to the digital logs.

The second investigator flipped the page forward, tracking the timeline back to the initial data intercept point in the central capital district. He shook his head, highlighting the text with his thumb.

"Let's establish the exact baseline for the surveillance files on the residential wiretap logs again," the second investigator insisted, reading directly from the primary evidence list.

CHAPTER TWO

The tape recorder continued to spin, but the dynamic in the small interrogation room was shifting. The focus turned from the technical architecture of the wireless tracking teams to the raw, visceral reality of the field operations.

"As the director of the DEA, shouldn't you have known about this corruption?" a senator's sharp voice echoed from a digital playback file on the investigator's tablet.

On the screen, a high-ranking official shifted uncomfortably in a congressional hearing seat. "Agents were cutting corners and engaging in prostitution in foreign countries," the official

countered defensively, his eyes darting toward the committee panel.

Hammon watched the video snippet play out, a grim smile touching his lips. He looked at the investigators across the table.

"Pretending to be a bad cop or a criminal is not as easy as it sounds," Hammon said, his voice dropping into a raspy whisper.

"My only job was to pretend to be dirty. I knew I was being followed and my phones were tapped. I had to convince the real bad cops I was one of them. If they smelled even a hint of hesitation, you don't just get burned—you vanish."

The lead investigator leaned forward, tapping his pen on his legal pad. "Walk us through the mechanics of the field rip-offs."

"For months we followed suspects using GPS trackers on their vehicles," Hammon explained, his eyes locking onto the lens of the recording camera. "Once these suspects leave their home, we kicked in the door and robbed them for everything. Adrenaline rushed through my body knowing how much danger we were in. On one specific hit, nearly $800k was in the home. Everything was being documented using my hidden cameras."

"And the other officers on your team?" Miller asked, his hand flying across his notebook. "Did they have any idea?"

"The crimes these officers were committing seemed second nature," Hammon said, shaking his head.

"They could care less if someone saw them. They operated with total impunity because they believed the badge made them invisible. Aerial surveillance watched over me just in case these officers figured out I was working with The Department of Justice.

Every afternoon I looked over my shoulder, because I didn't know if someone had made me."

Hammon leaned back, the metal chair scraping loudly against the concrete floor. The coldness of the interrogation room seemed to fade, replaced by the suffocating memories of the years he spent living a double life.

"Many days, sitting in this cell I had nightmares thinking of the crimes that were committed against innocent civilians," Hammon murmured, staring blankly at the gray wall. "I've watched dirty cops frame innocent men, and I couldn't do anything to stop it, because it would blow my cover. Civilians recorded me calling me all types of names, and I couldn't say anything. In their eyes I was a dirty cop too."

The lead investigator remained silent, letting the tape roll.

"Everything I did was to further the investigation," Hammon continued, his voice hardening. "My job was to bust dirty cops no matter what it takes. I have it on video. Federal agents gave informants listening devices to strap to their chest, in order to record suspects."

Suddenly, Hammon leaned forward, a dark, manipulative glint in his eyes. He looked directly at the lead investigator. "Everything I've told them was a story I made up."

The room went dead silent. The lead investigator blinked, his pen freezing mid-stroke.

"Well, at this point they really want you off the street,"

Miller stated, breaking the silence as he leaned over his file, his voice tight with an underlying warning. "And they are willing to do anything in order to make that happen."

The second investigator closed his folder with a heavy thud, looking up at the ceiling lights. The scale of the institutional decay went far beyond a single rogue undercover operation. It reached the very foundation of the legal system in Union South.

"We need to protect American citizens from big government," the second investigator muttered, almost to himself. "The Fourth Amendment is vanishing."

"It's already gone," Hammon countered flatly. "The Office of the Inspector General has opened an investigation into the DEA agents listed. But it's a smoke screen. A public relations move."

The lead investigator pulled up a separate congressional transcript, pointing to a classified section. "Who authorized the USSA Warrant?"

On the official record, the question from the senate floor had been met with a wall of bureaucratic stone. *"Senator, at this time I'm unable to disclose that information,"* the director's response read. *"I can assure you the Department of Justice was aware of the warrant."*

The narrative shifts from the sterile confines of the capital interrogation complex to a quiet neighborhood in the Americana district, where the fallout of the surveillance web was actively collapsing. Manny was a retired policeman who lived above a pizzeria, owned by a purchaser of a currency machine.

The smell of baked dough and old brick filled his small apartment. He had spent his retirement trying to distance himself from the politics of the precinct, but the wires running through the city infrastructure always had a way of tracing back to old assets.

The phone on Manny's kitchen counter buzzed sharply. He picked it up, recognizing the voice on the other end instantly.

"There are two federal agents waiting outside your door," the voice whispered, tight with urgency.

Manny froze, his eyes shifting toward the deadbolt lock on his front entrance. "For what?"

"They are here to see you."

The interrogation tape continued to roll, the tiny spools collecting the legacy of a career built on manufactured guilt. Hammon leaned his forearms on the cold steel table, his eyes drilling into the lead investigator. He wasn't just talking about abstract networks anymore; he was detailing the exact moment the rot consumed his unit from the inside out.

"Once I take a dime, I can't get out!"

Hammon's voice echoed his old partner's panic, his words cutting sharp into the silence of the room. He was remembering the night the threshold was crossed.

"You would rather let your family suffer than take a chance?" his partner had shot back, her voice tight with desperate ambition.

"If I get caught, you would surely suffer," Hammon had warned.

He looked across the table at Miller, shaking his head. "With that, there was no turning back. My ex-partner began living the upper-middle-class life almost overnight. The first thing she wanted was weight-loss surgery. Before you knew it, they'd spent almost $80,000.00 in a very short time. A quick IRS audit would reveal that this money was coming from some other place than law enforcement. You can't hide that kind of money on a civil servants salary."

The lead investigator tapped his pen against the edge of the recording module. "And that's when the infrastructure started cracking?"

"Worse," Hammon said. "Word is that the Department of Justice wants access to all the records pertaining to our evidence room.

The panic inside the precinct was immediate. One of the shift leads came to me white as a sheet and said, *'We have a problem. Real drugs were replaced with sheetrock.'* The order from the top was simple: *'Stall them, as long as you can.'"*

Hammon leaned completely back, his hands interlaced behind his head. The grim reality of the cover-up was far more violent than the paperwork.

"Surveillance turned into overdrive as dirty cops began robbing drug dealers to replace the stolen drugs missing from the evidence room," Hammon explained, his eyes cold. "They were ripping off active blocks just to get enough raw weight to repackage and restock the shelves before the federal auditors showed up with their scales."

Miller looked up from his legal pad, his face tense. "Did they pull it off?"

"Once one of the dealers ended up dead, all bets were off," Hammon stated flatly. "Someone figured out there was a dirty federal agent robbing drug dealers that just committed murder. The street network isn't stupid. They tracked the badges back to the source. Suddenly, it hit the wires. Breaking news: police are searching cars without a warrant looking for this agent. The warning went out across every tactical frequency—this agent is not rational, he is very unpredictable."

Hammon took a slow, deep breath, staring directly at the recording lens.

"The DEA, which was established in 1989, had become one of the government's embarrassments and a waste of resources. Whenever I got too close to an informant, they would disappear. Corrupt federal agents were using informants as double agents in order to sell narcotics, and someone had figured it out. They just didn't know who. The Attorney General began an investigation into dirty agents when one of the informants who disappeared was killed."

The perspective shifts from the secure interrogations of the capital to the frantic rhythm of the city streets.

At the downtown office of the 12 News Network, John sat at his desk, his computer monitors displaying a grid of open public records requests. His desk phone rang, an unlisted internal extension.

He picked up the receiver.

"12 News Network, this is John."

"John, you don't know me, but I know you," a distorted voice crackled over the line.

John frowned, leaning closer to the phone. "Who is this?"

"You are under surveillance," the caller whispered urgently. "The FBS has aerial vehicles including drones following you as we speak. Don't look out the window. Don't worry about who I am. When your waiter comes, your food is going to be in a to-go box with a phone inside. Don't open it until you get home. I'll call you in 10 minutes. Get rid of your phone."

The line went dead. John felt a cold sweat break out across the back of his neck. He paid his bill, grabbed the cardboard box from the counter, and walked out of the restaurant with his eyes in the sky the entire time. Every shadow between the storefronts felt like a lens.

Ten minutes later, inside the privacy of his living room, the burner phone inside the food box buzzed. John answered it immediately.

"John, I'm an undercover agent who was ordered to pretend to be dirty, and I now realize I'm being framed," Hammon's voice came through the small speaker, sharp and clear.

"Why would they frame you?" John asked, his investigative instincts taking over.

"Because I didn't go along with the corruption," Hammon replied. "Look, I have thousands of hours of audio and video as proof, and no one knows. Open your food all the way and there is a USB in it, with snippets of some of the videos. I need your word, John, that you will expose these dirty cops before they set me up."

John looked down at the silver drive resting against the paper packaging. "I'll look at it, and get back to you."

"You can't call me," Hammon said. "I'll call you."

John leaned his shoulder against the archive shelf, looking down at the legal timelines spread across the table. The strategy of the Department of Justice wasn't just aggressive—it was designed to be permanent.

"Prosecutors deliberately entrapped individuals in case their original charge didn't stick," John explained to his editor, his finger tracing a line on the court docket. "They had other charges for a later date waiting in reserve. If a target managed to beat the initial indictment in court, the feds simply pulled a secondary file out of their drawer."

The editor frowned, adjusting his glasses. "What happens if the clock runs out on those secondary files?"

"When the statute of limitations ran out, they would devise a new plan and strategize to get these same individuals on new crimes with longer statute of limitations," John said flatly. "They would engineer entirely new scenarios, manufacturing a fresh intersection with a federal law just to reset the clock. Nobody gets off the hook once the internet tracking team puts them in the database."

John gathered the papers into his briefcase and looked his editor directly in the eye. "I have one request."

"What is it?" the editor asked.

"I have a source that has been documenting police corruption for years, and I want to bring him on," John said.

The editor sighed, leaning back in his executive chair. "What's the problem?"

"He's a convicted felon and he wants to be paid cash only," John stated cleanly. "No type of trail."

The editor didn't hesitate, shaking his head instantly. "It'll never happen."

The scene cuts back sharply to the sterile, gray atmosphere of the capital interrogation room. The tape recorder spooled forward, registering a new line of tactical questioning from the lead investigator."Agent Hammon, were criminals the only people targeted?" the lead investigator asked.

"No," Hammon replied, his voice echoing slightly against the concrete walls.

"Can you tell us how you targeted individuals?"

Hammon shifted in his steel chair, looking directly into the recording lens. "If we find out someone has been in trouble before, they were easy targets. The system leaves a permanent digital footprint. It doesn't matter how long ago it was."

The second investigator leaned over his legal pad. "Did some of these individuals turn their lives around?"

"A lot of them did," Hammon admitted without a shred of remorse.

"What was the justification?" the lead investigator pressed.

"Many were business owners, and most didn't trust banks," Hammon explained, his voice matter-of-fact. "They kept physical cash on hand to run their operations—legitimate cash. But because they had an old record, we could easily flag the currency as suspected drug proceeds and seize it under civil forfeiture laws. They couldn't fight it without exposing their past."

The second investigator tapped his pen against the metal table. "How much money do you think you've stolen over the years?"

"We've stolen millions of dollars," Hammon said flatly.

"How much did you personally get?" the lead investigator asked, his eyes narrowing.

"About six hundred thousand dollars."

"What did you do with the money?"

"Paid bills, bought cars, bought rental property," Hammon recited, listing the assets like a routine grocery list.

The lead investigator leaned closer into the light. "How much do you think you have left?"

"I would say about three hundred thousand."

The second investigator flipped his folder to a highly sensitive public relations file, sliding a printed screenshot across the scratched steel table toward the former agent.

" There was a video online of an elderly lady crying because she was robbed by dirty cops," the second investigator said, his tone turning cold.

"Was that your team?"

"Yes," Hammon said without blinking.

The lead investigator slammed his hand flat on the table, his composure breaking for a fraction of a second. "Why would you target a grandmother?"

Hammon leaned forward, his face inches from the lead investigator's, his voice dropping into a chillingly logical register.

"She had a theft charge about thirty years earlier," Hammon whispered. "So we could easily say she profited from a crime. The system doesn't care about age, and it doesn't care about time. An old file is an open door."

The Assistant United States Attorney (AUSA) offered her a proffer to tell the prosecutor everything she knows. A proffer is pitched as a lifeline, a formal sit-down where a target can lay out their cards in exchange for leniency. But in the architecture of federal prosecution, a proffer is a tightening noose. Someone who is a liar should never sit down with an experienced attorney and say anything without a lawyer. Without a legal shield, every word spoken is a brick used to build an indictment.

Inside the quiet conference room of the federal office, the AUSA laid out a blank legal pad. Ms. Smith sat across from her, the weight of the investigation pressing down on her shoulders.

"Ms. Smith, can you give us all the information you have on your ex?" the AUSA asked, her voice deceptively warm.

Ms. Smith wrung her hands, staring down at the polished wood table. "I really don't know where to start."

"Tell us about his friends and relatives," the AUSA prompted smoothly.

Ms. Smith shook her head, her voice cracking under the tension. "I can't. I have no idea who they are."

But the room was a psychological pressure cooker. Federal agents pressured her for so long she told everything she knew that would later convict her. For eleven hours they asked questions that would entrap her no matter the answer.

Every denial was carved into an obstruction; every memory lapse was documented as a deliberate omission.

Federal agents don't record interviews with witnesses; they write down the information on FD-602's. The raw audio is never preserved for the defense to audit. If the investigators lie, you can't prove it unless you recorded it yourself. The FD-602 becomes the absolute truth in the eyes of the court, a manufactured script designed to fit the prosecution's narrative.

Witnesses are forced to wear wires in order to entrap individuals, regardless of their crime, in order to free themselves of prosecution.

The system loops back on itself: to save your own skin, you must become the camera that destroys someone else.

Back in the gray interrogation cell, Hammon watched the recording red light blink. His confession was expanding, moving from simple physical corruption to the deliberate psychological destruction of American citizens.

"For years, I participated in illegal surveillance orchestrated by the Justice Department," Hammon stated, his voice flat, devoid of the weight of what he was admitting. "Suspects' phones were tapped, and any website they visited or email they read, I was able to see it. I was able to follow my enemy day in and day out."

Miller stopped typing, looking up. "And that was legal under the initial routing?""Under federal guidance, I assumed I was exempt from prosecution because I was a good guy,"

Hammon said, a bitter edge cutting through his tone. "We all did. I was trained to manipulate the target and psychologically defeat them. My job was to lie and turn every associate of the target against them."

He leaned closer to the metal table, his eyes drilling into the lead investigator.

"You don't just lock them up. You dismantle them before they ever see a courtroom. Destroy their relationship with their job; if they are self-employed, take away their customers. Cut off all access to financial success and set them up for failure. Divide and conquer every relationship the suspect has in order to get them to submit. By the time they get to trial, they are broke, isolated, and mentally broken."

The lead investigator tapped his folder. "And if the evidence didn't support that level of intervention?"

"Federal agents who lied on government documents also lied to the grand jury," Hammon countered instantly. "The paperwork is easily cleaned up. If you can convince a court that the security of the nation is under threat, you don't need a warrant. The word 'security' is a skeleton key that unlocks every door in Americana."

Outside the federal buildings, the panic on the streets of the capital was turning raw. John's telephone line hummed with the voices of desperate targets who had finally realized they were living inside a digital panopticon.

"Man, I'm having trouble with dirty cops! How should I proceed?" a panicked source told John over an encrypted frequency.

"What kind of trouble?" John asked, recording the call from his home office.

"They are the kind that frame the innocent with crimes," the source breathed, the background noise echoing with city traffic. "I'm tired of the threats."

Suspects were fully aware they were under investigation, and didn't hide the fact they knew. The system had become so loud, so pervasive with drones and local tails, that the targets could see the wires. But knowing didn't save them.

Informants were given green lights to frame, if needed, any subject of an investigation. If a target was too clean, the informant's job was to fix it.

Up in the tactical coordination rooms of the tracking team, the surveillance layout was live. Monitors tracked a target pulling into a local service station.

"Target is talking to someone at the gas station," the field monitor reported over the encrypted channel. "Can we get a helicopter closer in to see who it is?"

The secondary radar sweep pulled up a blurry visual of the passenger side door. "We've never seen him before. Can we get a tail on him?"

The government not only investigates the target, it also investigates the target's friends. They leave no stone unturned; if there is wrongdoing, they will find it. And if they can't find it, they manufacture it.

The final section of the unredacted transcript detailed the direct testimony of a flipped informant standing before the federal grand jury, exposed by John's ongoing investigation into the customization shop network.

The prosecutor stood at the podium, looking at the witness on the stand. "Can you tell the Grand Jury what you were ordered to do once you entered the target's car?"

The witness cleared his throat, his voice amplification echoing through the secured courtroom. "I was told to steal his key signal, in order to later go back and plant narcotics in the vehicle."

The prosecutor leaned forward. "Were you able to do it?"

"No," the witness replied.

"Why?"

The informant looked directly at the grand jurors, exposing the flaw in the tracking team's digital architecture. "We later found out the vehicle had hidden cameras that were recording in and out of the vehicle. The target had back-stopped his own car. If we touched the lock signal, the data was already streaming to an off-site cloud server."

The lead investigator dropped a fresh, unredacted data ledger onto the scratched steel table. The room was cold, the internal air system vibrating the heavy metal walls.

"If you have to go to prisons and interview people, I want everything on these guys," the lead investigator ordered sharply, leaning over the paperwork.

The second investigator shook his head, staring at a monitor displaying flatlined audio waves. "We are running voice prints twenty-four seven, and are yet to pick up any conversation."

"What if he is disguising his voice or speaking another language?" the lead investigator muttered, tracing a timeline with his pen.

"That could be the reason we can't pick up on anything," the second investigator replied, adjusting his glasses. He sighed, rubbing his temples in frustration. "Had this been Joe Blow from up the street with no financial resources, he would have been indicted in a heartbeat. Instead, we're chasing a ghost."

Hammon let out a dry, cynical laugh from his side of the table.

"That's the playbook. Law enforcement can be on video beating and killing a man, and the prosecutor will take six months to investigate and find the officer feared for his life. But a civilian? A man can be accused of selling drugs, never caught with drugs or marked money, and found guilty, because a rat testified in court.

We pressured informants to lie on people we clearly knew were innocent of charges brought against them."

The lead investigator clicked his pen, turning his eyes back to the recorded log. "Let's get back to your specific directive under the Department of Justice."

"My only job was to pretend to be dirty, to uncover corruption," Hammon stated smoothly, his voice flat. "The Justice Department brought me in once they figured some of the agents were corrupt. But instead of throwing out the information that was already gathered, we were in constant contact with informants listening to every word the target said."

The second investigator flipped the page, tracking the failed wiretap logs of the tracking team.

"Can you get him to talk about crimes?" the lead investigator had asked the field team weeks prior.

"I can't get him to talk at all," the field monitor had reported back.

Hammon leaned forward, his face cutting through the glare of the overhead light. "We tried to get this guy on pimping charges, drug charges, extortion, wire fraud, theft—and nothing worked. He was not interested in crimes. The system kept pushing, searching for a single crack in the armor."

"Once again, he's one step ahead of us," the second investigator murmured, looking at the logs. "Or is he really not committing crimes?"

The lead investigator stood up, his face tight with executive authority. "I want every agent on this case to take a lie detector test."Miller blinked, startled. "For what?"

"To weed out any corruption," the lead investigator barked. "The government contractor is flying down tomorrow to demonstrate the new technology, and we want everyone cleared of any wrongdoing. I won't have this unit compromised before the presentation."

The second investigator tapped his legal pad nervously. "What if the technology just doesn't work?"

"If that's the case, all of our phones and the phones of our family members are compromised," the lead investigator stated flatly.

A heavy silence fell over the interrogation room. Miller lowered his pen, looking between Hammon and his partner. "What if they are doing to us what we do to them?"

The lead investigator frowned. "What do you mean?"

"Listening to our conversations with our wives, knowing where we are going, having our contact list," Miller whispered, his eyes wide.

"It's possible, but unlikely," the lead investigator dismissed, though his voice lacked conviction.

"What if they can see everything we are doing?"

"They can't," the lead investigator snapped. He leaned over the table, his posture turning aggressively tactical. "Get the word out that we are about to start an investigation.

Tell every informant something different; once it comes back to us, we will know exactly where it came from."

"And if they don't fall for it?" Miller asked.

"Then we know it's not the informants," the lead investigator said coldly. "Either they see and hear everything we do, or they don't. The likelihood of these guys giving information to a complete

stranger is small. We just need to be on our toes. Bring in a new undercover female, fresh out of the FBS academy."

He gestured to the secondary asset sheet. "Give her a cover story. Get her into the clubs, find out who the ballers are. Find a way to connect these guys to a crime. If you can't, create a crime. Find a mistress—anything of value to hold over their head."

Hammon shook his head, staring at his chained hands. "At this time, I started to realize we weren't investigating crimes; we were setting individuals up. I think it was clear that these guys aren't as dumb as they look, and they could see everything we were planning. The prosecutors were orchestrating these setups, and I couldn't prove it without recording it. Every meeting, I was searched for bugging devices, so there was no way to record the conversation."

CHAPTER THREE

John's investigation outside the complex was pulling the same thread from the opposite end. Using a intercepted IMSI catcher log, his news team had managed to decrypt a highly sensitive series of conversations.

Through the black-market signal receiver, they were able to pick up a conversation from a federal inmate who continually claimed he was framed by dirty cops. The data was crystal clear, revealing a terrifying reality that the federal unit had completely missed.

The entire time that we were watching them, they were watching us. Our surveillance had been blown years ago, and we didn't know it. We were building a case against them, and they were building a case against dirty cops.

Inside the visiting module of the maximum-security wing, two connected assets sat behind the scratched plexiglass, talking through the secured landline receivers.

"Instead of following me, they should spend that time drawing up letters to send to defense attorneys," the inmate muttered, his eyes scanning the guard towers.

"They aren't going to believe us," his contact replied through the phone. "We have to prove it."

"How?"

"Start with the overtime theft," the contact whispered. "That's where the paper trail breaks down."

"How can we trust a cop who steals and has a mistress?" the inmate countered bitterly, looking down at his orange jumpsuit.

The contact pressed his hand against the glass. "Keep your head up. We are working to get you out."

Back in the coordinator's office, the field supervisor reviewed the extraction protocols for the secure cellblocks.

"My job was to find out every inmate he had a conversation with, and pull them one by one," the supervisor's field notes recorded. "We couldn't get them all out for attorney visits, so we would use medical reasons in order to get them out."

Inside the private, concrete examination room of the infirmary, an FBS handler stood across from a flipped inmate who had been pulled from his cell under a fake medical transport order.

"You know why we are here," the handler said, keeping his voice low.

"Yes, but what do I get out of it?" the inmate replied, crossing his arms.

"We can move you closer to your family," the handler offered smoothly.

The inmate let out a harsh, quiet laugh, leaning closer. "Look, this whole compound is wired. They can hear everything."The handler froze. "What do you mean?"

"Man, they know everything," the inmate whispered, his eyes darting to the vents.

"Like what?"

"They know where guards live, who they associate with, and what they eat for breakfast."

The handler's heart hammered against his ribs. "How are they getting this information?"

"One of your agents, a female DEA agent, has kids with one of the guys," the inmate revealed, a sharp smile touching his lips.

The handler leaned in, his voice tight. "Do you know anything else about her?"

"No," the inmate said, shaking his head. "Just that she doesn't work for the DEA anymore."

"Do you know why?"

"She exposed corruption and was fired," the inmate said flatly. "Do you know—"

The handler leaned closer, the harsh fluorescent lighting of the infirmary casting long shadows over the inmate's face. "Do you know anything else?"

"They always talk about smoke detectors and needle pins, I don't know what it means," the inmate whispered, his voice barely audible over the hum of the prison's cooling unit.

The handler's chest tightened. For the first time, we were able to see what was going on. They had cameras placed in smoke detectors of agents' homes and the homes of informants. The realization swept through the upper echelons of the tracking team like a contagion. Agents were nervous because they didn't know what was captured on the videos. Suspected criminals were using our techniques against us.

We didn't know whose cover was blown or who was corrupt. From that interview on, we couldn't get anything else on wiretap.

The channels went cold, the frequencies flatlining one by one. They knew we talked to this inmate, and he was moved immediately for safety reasons.

"We suspected the guards were on the payroll, but it was no way to prove it," Hammon noted bitterly from his side of the interrogation table. "Just like that, all communication stopped."

Miller stared down at his notebook, his hand frozen. "I have no idea what happened."

"We can't rule anything out," the lead investigator stated, his voice flat and hard. "We have to assume our car, our homes, and even our offices are bugged."

Miller looked up, a trace of exhaustion breaking through his professional mask. "Why go through so much trouble?"

"This is out of my pay grade," the lead investigator snapped.

The lead investigator paced the length of the concrete room, his fingers tapping against his thigh. He stopped by the metal table, slamming a blank affidavit down.

"Can we get a warrant for 24-hour surveillance?" Miller asked.

"As long as they are in public, we don't need a warrant," the lead investigator explained coldly. "If they are in private residences, we will kick in the national security threat."

Miller frowned, looking at the paperwork. "National Security Threat?"

"If we say that American citizens are being threatened, we can get an emergency warrant," the lead investigator replied.

"But it wouldn't be true," Miller countered, his voice tightening.

"They don't know that! The USSA court has a rubber stamp, and we can get a warrant if we swear to it."

Miller pushed his chair back, shaking his head. "I can't lie to the court."The lead investigator leaned down, his eyes narrowing into slits, his posture turning predatory. "We need you to do it, this one time."

"I can't," Miller said.

Hammon watched the standoff from across the table, a dark, heavy understanding washing over him. If they didn't know I was working with the Department of Justice, they know now.

"I was the weak link, and now I had a target on my back,"

Hammon murmured, his mind flashing back to the immediate retaliation that followed his internal reports. "Dead rats were placed in my locker, my personal car tires were flat, and my home was painted with derogatory names. I couldn't trust anyone. I thought everyone was out to get me, even though I was trying to do the right thing. The same people who I thought were there to protect me were actually plotting to deceive me. Hammon shifted the weight of his cuffs, the metal clinking against the steel table.

"We have a Title 3 wiretap authorization."

The investigators remained quiet, allowing the recording tape to capture every word.

"I listened to thousands of calls every week," Hammon continued. "From conspiracy theorists to individuals who thought birds were equipped with spy cameras. The noise was constant. But then you catch the clear frequencies. You catch the people who actually know they are being hunted."

The scene cuts to an intercepted phone log, the digital waveform pulsing sharply as two targets connected on an unencrypted local line.

“Hello,” the first voice came through the speaker.

“What’s going on?” the second asked.

“Nothing much.”

“I see you have company,” the first voice noted, a casual rhythm to his words that defied the weight of the situation.

“Yeah, they’ve been following me for about a week.”

“Well, that’s not all. There’s an informant working at your shop.”

The line quieted for a beat before the second voice sighed. “We figured that.”

Deep within the internet tracking unit, the console screens pulsed with real-time metadata. An analyst hit a sequence on his keyboard, bringing up a live intercept map of Americana's central district.

"We can access the camera as well," the analyst muttered, dragging a cursor over a high-definition video feed.

"I think he knows the capabilities we have," the field supervisor replied, leaning over the analyst's shoulder.

The analyst brought up an encrypted data package extracted from an active cell trap. "His contact list has John from 12 News Network in it."

The supervisor's face tightened. "Turn on the mic on his phone, and see what's going on. Why would he be talking to an investigative journalist?"

The analyst clicked through the audio matrix, attempting to establish a stable stream. "Do you think it's possible they are investigating dirty cops?"

Before the supervisor could answer, a completely separate, encrypted line rang on the master console. It was a restricted channel reserved for street-level intelligence. The supervisor punched the speaker button.

"Hello," the supervisor barked.

"This is CI 49," a frantic voice crackled over the line.

"What you got?"

"You are not going to believe this, but they are recording you guys investigating them," the informant whispered, the background noise echoing with the rush of city traffic.

The supervisor let out a harsh, disbelieving laugh. "What do you mean?"

"They have people out recording police following them."

"You're kidding."

"No, it's even worse," CI 49 pushed, his voice trembling. "They have cameras hidden at intersections, parks, and police stations."

The supervisor stood up straight, a cold sweat breaking out across his forehead. "How do you know this?"

"Because I saw you leave your house, and there is a camera on the street light outside your house," the informant revealed.

The supervisor gripped the edge of the console. "What else?"

"They have a murder caught on one of the videos that a cop committed, and an innocent man is doing time for it," CI 49 stated flatly.

The supervisor's breath hitched. "They have a murder on tape?"

"Yes. From the look of it, these guys have been watching you investigate them for years."

"That's impossible!" the supervisor snapped, slamming his hand onto the desk.

"Man, I saw what I saw," the informant argued. "I watched a rookie cop go from a full head of hair to completely bald on their monitoring timeline. These guys are the real deal. They hate dirty cops."

The supervisor closed his eyes, trying to calculate the absolute failure of his perimeter security. "Do you know anything else?"

"One of them is an ex-DEA agent fired for turning on a fellow agent," CI 49 said.

"An ex-DEA agent?"

"It's safe to say that most of them are ex-military or law enforcement."

The leak was real. Although it wasn't clear who it was, someone from law enforcement was sending these guys information on

dirty cops. Case after case had information about witnesses forced to lie or fabricate testimony. The targets had built an mirror image of the federal intelligence apparatus.

Inside an undisclosed briefing room, two senior investigators stared at a leaked dossier they had intercepted from an encrypted cloud server.

"If you look at the first file, that is a shield that I have never seen," the first investigator noted, pointing to an unfamiliar tactical emblem printed at the top of the unredacted documents.

"I'm pretty sure it's the USSA," the second investigator replied, adjusting his glasses.

"I thought that also, but it's not," the first investigator countered grimly. "It's not even funny. There are people in prison who shouldn't be."

The second investigator sighed, scrolling through page after page of falsified arrest records. "I don't see how someone can knowingly send an innocent man to prison from evidence from a dirty cop."

"The jail is full of them, we will never know how many," the first investigator said flatly. "Anyway, have our guys look over the first file. There are some interesting names on it."

The second investigator pointed to a list of high-ranking regional directors. "I have no idea how these agents weren't impeached years ago."

"It's not about who's right or wrong, it's about conviction rates," the first investigator explained, his voice hollow. "The best thing to do is not let anyone know you're onto them. Let them think you have no idea you're being followed. Once they know that you know, they will change their tactics. Don't be surprised if people you haven't seen in years all of a sudden start showing up in unexpected places."

The strategy was absolute. The same way law enforcement had organizational charts, they were using organizational charts to identify dirty cops.

The rot ran deep into the past. A reporter was killed years earlier, even though the coroner reported it as a suicide. No one could prove the cover-up, but everyone suspected foul play. It was a repeating pattern in Americana: an individual has no previous mental issues, and all of a sudden commits suicide after exposing corruption.

John, with 12 News Network, began his own investigation into people who were previously incarcerated, and found they all had the same story.

They were convicted felons or people not in good standing in the community, and no one would believe anything they said. Some were homeless, others were impoverished, and they saw a way out by becoming government informants. The Bureau used their desperation as raw material. Some of these individuals didn't even know what the suspects looked like; they were just told to point out the person at the defense table.

The memory of the prep sessions echoed through the legal files John uncovered.

"When you get in the court, just point out the person at the defense table," the handler had instructed an informant inside a holding cell.

"What if they don't believe me?" the informant had asked nervously.

"They will, we are the government."

"What if the defense finds out I lied? The judge will put me in jail."

"We won't prosecute you," the handler reassured with a cold smile. "All you need to say is you've been knowing him for years, and he's the fence for stolen goods."

The climax of John's investigation culminated inside the wood-paneled walls of the Americana Federal Courthouse. The defense attorney stood at the podium, facing the government's star informant on the witness stand.

"CI 3129, how do you know my client?" the defense attorney asked, his voice sharp.

"I sold him stolen goods for years," the informant stated, reciting the rehearsed script.

"Can you give us his phone number?"

The informant blinked, shifting in the seat. "No, I don't know it."

"So, how did you contact him?"

"I would go to his house."

"Where did he live?" the defense attorney pressed, stepping closer to the box.

"I don't remember."

"If you had stolen goods, would you remember?"

"He is the person I sold stolen goods to," the informant insisted, his eyes darting toward the prosecutor's table.

"Tell the court all the places you've met my client to sell stolen goods?"

"It was many."

"How did you contact him?"

"By phone."

The defense attorney pulled a thick binder from his table. "CI 3129, you do know we have your phone records, right?"

"Yes."

"Show the court which number is my client's."

The informant sweated under the glare of the courtroom lights. "I'm not sure."

"We were able to identify every number on your phone, and not one was associated with my client," the defense attorney declared loudly, turning toward the jury box.

"That's not true."

"Well, show us."

The informant swallowed hard, his voice cracking. "I called him from a pay phone."

"Give us a location to the pay phone."

"I don't remember."

The defense attorney leaned in, his expression turning entirely uncompromising. "CI 3129, are you a crack head?"

"Objection!" the prosecutor shouted, standing up sharply.

"I withdraw, Your Honor," the defense attorney countered smoothly, without breaking eye contact with the witness. "Are you a dope fiend?"

"Objection!"

The judge slammed his gavel down. "Court is in recess."

Inside the judge's chambers during the emergency hearing, the gloves came off completely.

"Your Honor, the government has solicited known drug addicts to turn state's evidence against my client," the defense attorney argued fiercely. "Furthermore, these same addicts have admitted to individuals that the government has paid their living expenses for the last six weeks."

The prosecutor stood straight, his expression rigid. "Your Honor, we wanted to keep this informant on ice, so we paid for his hotel to keep him close by for trial."

"Your Honor, the government is using this case to get my client to roll over on another defendant that is awaiting trial," the defense attorney shot back, gesturing toward the courtroom door. "My client is a businessman with no criminal record, and the only people the government can get to say something disparaging are career criminals and drug addicts."

The prosecutor leaned forward, tapping his fingers on the judge's desk. "Your Honor, there are things we can't disclose because of the States Secret Act."

"Your Honor, the government is bringing in the States Secret Act to shield itself from embarrassment!" the defense attorney shouted. "We have information on corruption all the way to the Department of Justice."

The judge held up a hand, silencing them both. "Court is in recess until Monday morning."

The weekend recess offered no relief. The government on numerous occasions tried to deceive the court with testimony from witnesses who were proven liars.

When the verbal ambushes failed in front of a jury, the field teams reverted to physical fabrication. Federal agents told informants to put drugs in defendants' cars. But the surveillance loop had already reversed. Security footage captured from nearby storefronts showed cars were broken into, and unknown suspects put something in those same cars that were pulled over by patrol cruisers minutes later. The setup was fully documented on digital tape.

Inside the defense war room, the attorney reviewed the security files with John.

"The judge is going to move in the Government's favor, so we need to be prepared for that," John warned, looking at the court precedents.

The defense attorney stared at the unredacted video of the frame-up. "I'm not sure about that."

On Monday morning, the gallery was packed to capacity. The air inside the courtroom was thick with anticipation. The judge took the bench, and the jury filed into their box.

"Good morning, jury," the judge announced.

"Good morning," the jurors replied in unison.

The judge turned his eyes toward the defense podium. "The defense will continue to cross-examine the state's witness."

The defense attorney stepped forward, his eyes locked onto the informant who had been returned to the witness stand. He didn't waste time with technicalities. He went straight for the baseline.

"CI 3129, do you do drugs?"

The informant looked down at his lap. "I have in the past."

"When was the last time you did drugs?"

"Months ago."

"So, if the court orders a drug test, would you pass?" the defense attorney asked, his voice echoing through the silent room. He stepped directly into the informant's line of sight, blocking his

view of the government's table. "Without looking at the prosecutor, tell the jury if you would pass."

The room held its breath. The informant's shoulders slumped. He looked away from the jury box.

"No," the informant whispered. "I wouldn't pass."

"So, why would you try and deceive the court?" the defense attorney demanded.

The informant cracked under the absolute weight of the exposure. He pointed a trembling finger across the room. "The prosecutor forced me to lie."

"Objection!" the prosecutor screamed, slamming his hands onto the table as he stood up.

The defense attorney didn't wait for the dust to settle. He turned directly to the bench, his voice echoing with absolute authority.

"Your Honor, the defense asks for a mistrial. The government's own witness said he was forced to lie."

The judge stared down at the prosecutor, then at the trembling informant, before hitting his gavel with an icy calmness.

"Request denied."

The judge's denial of a mistrial did not halt the momentum of the truth. Out on the streets and high in the stratosphere over

Americana, the architecture of the surveillance state continued to rotate.

CHAPTER FOUR

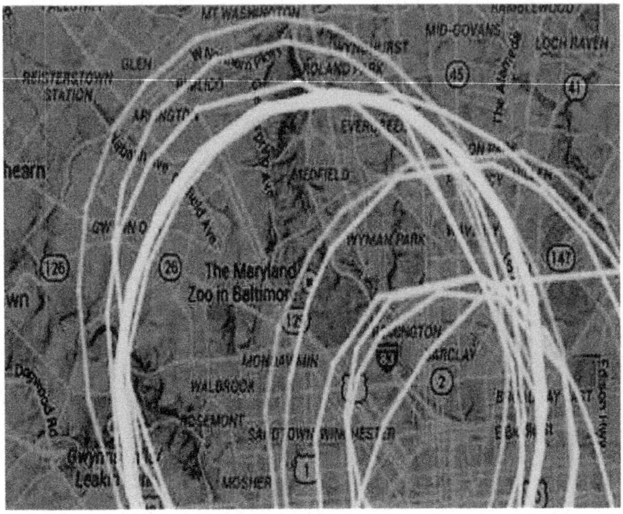

Flightradar24.com

Aerial vehicles are being deployed in cities across the country. Small planes are equipped with spy gear that pretend to be cell towers of legitimate cell phone companies. Day and night, these aircraft circle the city and capture thousands of subscribers' phone signals, metadata, and text messages. The extraction is indiscriminate, pulling the private data of everyone walking the streets below into a central net.

To keep the operation hidden from public oversight, the DEA began to paint the government planes the same as commercial planes, in order to disguise the flight plan from investigative reporters. The trickery kept the true nature of the fleet off the radars of independent watchdogs.

But the collection method goes far deeper than tracking frequencies. The same vehicles, equipped with infrared cameras, are patrolling the sky looking for heat signatures in vehicles and commercial buildings.

Planes are used with tower dumps and forensic software, in order to see what phones are pinging off a particular phone tower in a given time.

The tracking team operates without boundaries. Planes are being deployed to capture metadata in real time, even when specific targets' phones are off.

The battery pulse alone is enough to feed the software. Back inside the grey, reinforced interrogation room, the lead investigator adjusted the audio input levels of the recording console. He brought the debriefing back to the unchecked expansion of the aviation grid.

"Agent Hammon, can you explain how you were allowed to get so much access to aerial surveillance?" the lead investigator asked.

"We were doing investigations, therefore we needed them, because nothing else worked," Hammon explained, his voice entirely flat.

"What do you mean nothing else worked?" Miller asked, looking up from his legal pad.

"We couldn't get the phone signal from any of the targets," Hammon revealed. "We flew over homes of suspects daily to catch any type of correspondence. We couldn't let them out of our sight.

Once it became apparent that this prosecutor had it in for these guys, I had to do something."

The lead investigator leaned forward, his hands resting on the scratched steel table. "Did you notify your superiors that the targets were clean?"

"We kept telling him, they aren't committing crimes," Hammon said, shaking his head bitterly. "He said find something, anything just to get him something. The conviction rate was all that mattered to the office."

The second investigator turned to a highly sensitive, flagged section of the operational files. "Are you aware of any evidence holding?"

"Yes," Hammon said instantly.

"What evidence was withheld?" the lead investigator pressed.

"We had evidence another person committed a crime, and we were told to disregard that person and stick with the target suspect," Hammon admitted, exposing the deliberate frame-up.

The second investigator slid a heavily redacted personnel folder across the table toward the former agent. "At any time during your investigation, did someone present you with disciplinary files of anyone in law enforcement?"

"Yes," Hammon said, glancing down at the dark lines of marker crossing out the names.

"Can you tell me, what was in those files?"

Hammon hesitated, his fingers tracing the edge of the paper. "I'm not sure I can."

"Did anything in those files suggest corruption?" the lead investigator asked, leaning into the light.

"Everything in the files suggested corruption," Hammon stated plainly.

"Did any of the files have names of informants who worked with these corrupt cops?" Miller asked, his pen hovering.

"Yes."

The lead investigator clicked his pen against the desk. "Do you want to tell us about it?"

"I want to," Hammon whispered, his posture stiffening as he looked toward the security door. "I'm just afraid of what can happen to me."

"As long as you are truthful, you have nothing to be worried about," the lead investigator reassured him, though the promise rang hollow in the cold room.

Hammon let out a short, humorless breath. "The informants were incentivized, they had a reason to lie—either they were working off a case or wanted money."

"Can you prove it?" Miller asked.

"I witnessed federal agents threaten informants with jail or prison if they didn't lie about a suspect," Hammon revealed. "It's a factory of perjury."

The lead investigator checked a live intelligence feed on his tablet. "Are you aware that your old team is out now working this case?"

"I suspect they are," Hammon said, his voice dropping an octave. "They were told to stay on these guys twenty-four seven."

The scene cuts directly to the tactical communications frequency running live over the Americana transit corridors.

"Suspect is on the move, approaching 418 and 101," a surveillance unit reported over the encrypted channel.

"Copy," the command base replied.

"Can you get the license plate of the truck following behind?" the field agent asked, trying to read the vehicle through the glare of the streetlights.

"Can't read it. Send in local PD."

The network was seamless. Federal agents were working with local police departments in order to help with the federal task force. The local cruisers were used as the muscle, executing the physical stops while the feds remained in the shadows.

Back in the interrogation cell, the lead investigator pushed for the logistics of the flights. "How does it work?"

"We would meet at a particular airstrip and go over the day's plan," Hammon explained to the investigators.

"What would the plan consist of?" Miller asked.

"We were having trouble getting the cell phone locations from a particular suspect, so we would do circular routes over the area he was at and deploy the IMSI catcher," Hammon said.

The lead investigator crossed his arms, staring hard at the former agent. "A federal appeals court ruled that surveillance planes were unconstitutional."

"Well, we've been doing it for years," Hammon countered flatly, completely unfazed by the legal boundary.

"Can you tell me about the infrared cameras?" the second investigator asked.

"They were mostly used to search for illegal grow houses, then we began monitoring the inside of suspects' homes," Hammon revealed.

The lead investigator's face tightened with genuine shock. "So, you were able to see inside citizens' homes from the sky?"

"We could see everything they did in their home, from showering to cleaning dishes," Hammon stated smoothly, his voice dropping into a chillingly matter-of-fact register. "Look, my job was to pretend to be a dirty cop, so I had to play the part."

The lead investigator clicked his pen one final time, looking into the lens of the recording camera. "Clearly, laws were broken, and you were doing a search without a warrant."

The interrogation room seemed to constrict, the heavy gray walls absorbing the explosive weight of Hammon's continuing testimony. The spools of the recorder turned with a faint, rhythmic friction.

"We could hear up to thirty feet," Hammon stated, his voice chillingly calm as he described the capabilities of the low-altitude aircraft array.

The lead investigator lowered his pen, staring across the scratched metal table. "So you could hear inside the homes of people you think may be committing crimes, but you have no solid proof?"

"Yes," Hammon replied without a single flicker of hesitation. He leaned back, the chains of his cuffs clinking against the steel furniture. "We had planes flying over the homes of suspects twenty-four hours a day for years. Some we never indicted; we just had a feeling they were criminals. In the architecture of the tracking team, intuition was treated as probable cause.

If a regional director had a hunch, a target became a permanent fixture on our flight paths."

Miller swapped a tense glance with his partner, his fingers trembling slightly as he recorded the admission. "And the targets? Did they ever realize the scale of the net over their heads?"

"Most didn't," Hammon said, his eyes narrowing as his mind drifted back to the active logs. "But one particular suspect knew there were corrupt federal agents, and that's all he would talk about. He knew of specific cases, and this is when I began to be worried. He wasn't just guessing. He had the facts, the names, and the dates."

Hammon leaned his forearms back on the table, bringing his face into the sharp focus of the overhead lens.

"There was a conversation I will never forget," Hammon murmured, his voice dropping into a raspy whisper as he quoted the intercepted audio verbatim from memory. "The suspect was talking to a contact inside his residence, totally aware of the low-frequency drone above his roof.

He said, *'Innocent people are sitting in prison, and they are allowing this to happen. How can you knowingly take cases from dirty cops?'"*

The lead investigator remained completely silent, letting Hammon breathe through the memory.

"The suspect didn't stop there," Hammon continued, a grim smile breaking through his exhaustion. "He looked up at his ceiling and said into our microphones: *'Instead of following me around all day in these planes, they should be preparing letters to send to defense attorneys explaining their clients were wrongfully convicted."*

Miller cleared his throat, looking up from his legal pad. "What was the prosecutor's reaction when you delivered that transcript?"

"They laughed," Hammon said bluntly. "The consensus was absolute: *'They will never do that. They will hide it until it can't be hidden any longer. They know there are no consequences to their actions, so there's no need to come forward with these findings.'* But the suspect's contact had the final word on that tape. He told the suspect, *'If they don't come forward after finding out the cops were dirty, they are dirty too.'* And he was right. The whole department became an accessory to the frame-ups."

The scene cuts sharply away from the capital interrogation cells to the live, high-definition display inside an FBS tracking van parked three blocks from the Americana Financial Center.

"Suspect is going into the bank," the ground unit reported over the tactical frequency.

Up in the circling Cessna, an analyst punched the target's credentials into a commercial database. "Find out if he has a safety deposit box."

A beat of static cut through the line. "He does not."

"Why does he keep going to the same bank?" the ground unit muttered, watching the target walk through the glass double doors from across the street.

"Maybe someone in the bank is helping him," the aerial monitor suggested, pulling up the employee roster for that specific branch.

"Hold on, his digital signature just spiked. Someone is calling him now. Intercepting the audio track."

The waveform on the monitor split, delivering a clean stream of a live, encrypted cellular call.

"Hello," the target answered.

"Your boy is in a deposition, and he showed up with two lawyers," a strained voice warned on the other end.

The target stopped in the lobby of the bank. "You're kidding."

"No. He doesn't trust them. They tried to get him to lie on someone, and he knows they will lie on him also."

"Did they check him before he went into the room?" the target asked, his voice tightening.

"The video shows them patting him down in the parking lot," the caller revealed, referring to a hidden local camera feed. "He's an informant. They were making sure he doesn't have anything on him. No wire, no backup recorder, nothing that could expose the setup."

On the other side of the city, John sat in the passenger seat of a vehicle, his eyes tracking the wide, looping trajectory of a white twin-engine plane cutting through the low clouds. He held a modified satellite phone to his ear.

"There are planes circling me right now," John stated, his tone flat with investigative focus.

"Those are surveillance planes trying to steal your data," his contact replied instantly through the secured line. "Why do you think they want all the electronic devices from your home? It's not about finding contraband, John. It's in order to have all the evidence, and you have none proving your innocence. If they seize your drives, they control the narrative."

John reached down, tapping the heavy steel casing of a portable, military-grade storage unit resting between his feet.

"Like I said, there are no statute of limitations on murder, and a dirty cop committing a murder on video is like gold.

They can delete the digital files from their own secure servers, but they can't touch what they can't find."

"They are going to say the videos are doctored and made up," the contact warned. "The Department of Justice will bring in their own forensic experts to claim the frames were synthesized."

John unlocked the steel casing, revealing a set of heavy, magnetic tape reels resting safely within anti-static sleeves. "That's why we kept the original analog. You can't hack a physical strip of film. The light captured on those chemical grains is permanent."

High above the skyline, far out of sight of the common pedestrian, the hidden machinery of the state continued its silent sweep. Planes circle above entire cities day and night, capturing video and stealing data from unsuspecting citizens, building an infinite catalog of human movement, completely detached from the boundaries of the law.

The steady spool of the recording machine seemed to anchor the cold reality filling the interrogation room. Hammon looked from the spinning tape directly into the eyes of the lead investigator, his posture unyielding despite the steel cuffs anchoring him to the table.

"Hundreds of drones are launched every night to do mass surveillance," Hammon stated, his voice flat, completely stripped of any theatricality. "The sky over Americana isn't empty after dark. It's crawling with autonomous rotors. Land of the free is just a slogan; with artificial intelligence, license plate readers, and facial recognition, there is no way we are free."

Miller stopped his pen mid-sentence, looking up at the former agent. The weight of the admission seemed to chill the small concrete room.

"Everything we do is being recorded," Hammon continued, leaning forward until the harsh overhead light caught the deep lines of exhaustion on his face. "From social media to going to the grocery store, our every move is documented. Recent software can spot gunshots from miles away and alert law enforcement exactly where the gunshots came from. The infrastructure is seamless, Miller. Road deputies can pull over a traffic violator and extract all the information on his phone within seconds without ever unlocking the phone. The data is pulled right through the air before the driver even rolls down their window."

The lead investigator crossed his arms, his jaw tight. "And the legal challenges to those roadside extractions? The defense bar must be flooding the dockets with suppression motions."

Hammon let out a short, bitter chuckle. "Even if law enforcement is caught breaking the law and obtaining information without a warrant, the court will not charge them because of qualified immunity. The shield is absolute. The system protects its own hands, no matter how dirty they get."

The perspective cuts cleanly back to the busy, high-energy layout of the 12 News Network headquarters. John sat at his desk, a secure landline receiver pressed tightly against his ear while his computer screens blinked with incoming public record alerts. His assistant tapped on the glass door before stepping inside the office. "Your contact at the Office of the Inspector General is calling."

John didn't hesitate, gesturing toward the console. "Send her through."

A sharp click echoed over the digital line as the secure connection stabilized. "They are moving our guy out of solitary confinement," the OIG investigator whispered, her voice tight with professional caution. John leaned forward, his investigative instincts immediately tracking the tactical shift. "That's good news."

"I think they did it to see who he has contact with on the outside," she warned.

"I'm sure that's why they did it," John agreed, nodding slowly. "They're using his release as a homing beacon. They want to map out the network he's feeding information to. What else do you have from the central office?"

"Another thing," the contact noted, the sound of papers rustling faintly over the line. "They want more articles on dirty cops. The internal friction is building, John. The higher-ups need public pressure to force the department's hand."

John smiled, a grim, calculated expression. "No problem. I have them coming. Tonight, 12 News investigates dirty cops."

Later that afternoon, John met his senior broadcast editor in the dark, soundproof confines of the network's editing bay. The blue light of the monitors reflected off stacks of unredacted police disciplinary logs and hidden-camera tapes.

"What if the first video they show is a dirty cop in the back of the car stuffing money in his vest?" the editor asked, pointing to a paused frame on the master console.

John shook his head, staring at the raw footage of the precinct betrayal. "It'll never happen. The police will find some dirt on some editor, and it will disappear. They'll squeeze the board of directors before the broadcast signal even hits the tower."

"They might not have the leverage they think they do," the editor countered, pulling up a fresh police wire update. "One dirtbag killed himself last night because he found out they were going to indict him the following morning."

John's eyes hardened as he watched the digital ticker stream across the secondary screen. "That's crazy. Maybe more should kill themselves instead of robbing old ladies and framing innocent people."

"The panic inside the station is real, John. They know the walls are closing in."

"These cowards put pressure on innocent people, but can't take the same pressure put on them," John stated flatly, his voice echoing in the small room. He tapped the desk, gesturing to the recorded interrogation transcripts.

"You have to understand the tactics they are using in order to trick you. They sit in rooms with these prosecutors, and they tell them exactly what they need you to do so they can charge you with a crime. The entire operation is a pre-written script."

The air frequency above the city hummed with tense, rapid tactical reports. Inside the circling twin-engine surveillance plane, the analyst adjusted the focus of the high-definition thermal array, tracking red heat signatures moving through a residential corridor below.

"This doesn't sound right," the tactical coordinator muttered, leaning over the console with his headset pressed tightly to his ear.

"Can we get an aerial sniper?" the ground unit leader demanded over the encrypted frequency, his voice tight with panic. "They are running out the house!"

A chaotic burst of gunfire crackled across the channel, followed by sharp, breathless radio silence. Seconds later, a field agent's voice broke through the static, sounding completely unmoored. "We have a problem. We can't find any guns or drugs in the house."

The coordinator's face drained of color as he looked out the cabin window, spotting the distant, flashing rotors of local media helicopters rushing toward the perimeter. "Get those news choppers out of here!"

By sunset, the narrative was already being scrubbed, but the blood on Canal Street could not be hidden. Inside the 12 News Network editing bay, the broadcast monitors cut to a live remote feed.

"Breaking news at six," the anchor stated. "Five dead in an apparent botched raid on Canal Street."

The camera feed cut to the chaotic street corner, where flashing blue lights cut through the heavy evening mist.

John stood at the edge of the yellow crime scene tape, his digital recorder raised as the precinct captain attempted to slip past the crowd.

"The investigative reporter from twelve is here," a sergeant hissed into his shoulder mic. "Get him out of here."

John pushed forward, ignoring the officer who stepped in front of him. "Captain, can you tell us what's going on here?"

The captain stopped, his jaw tight, refusing to look directly into the camera lens. "This is an ongoing drug investigation."

"So, you found drugs in the house?" John demanded sharply.

"It's ongoing," the captain parried.

"Did you, or did you not find drugs?"

"Like I said, the investigation is ongoing."

John held his ground, his voice echoing over the noise of the idling emergency vehicles. "I don't think that's good enough. The people of this community would like to know if five innocent people were gunned down by a sniper in a helicopter?"

The captain glared at John, his expression turning icy. "No comment."

Months went by, and we listened to everything from illegal gambling to political corruption. The data net captured every transaction, every unlisted phone call, and every digital whisper inside the capital city. The tracking team watched from the sky as the mayor of the city was getting kickbacks from a developer and school board members.

"We did surveillance on the mayor," Hammon revealed to the investigators inside the gray debriefing room, "and the only thing we had on him was soliciting prostitution. None of the wiretaps ever had him saying anything illegal; the board members and the developer were a different story."

The lead investigator flipped a tab in the ledger. "How did they leverage it?"

"They were extorting the mayor because they knew he was seeing a prostitute," Hammon explained flatly. "The intercepted logs showed the developer outlining the exact parameters of the ambush. He told the board members:

'This is an elected official engaging in prostitution. He has no choice but to give us the contract or we will publicly humiliate him.' But one of the older board members hesitated. He said, *'I don't think it's that easy.'"*

Hammon leaned forward, his steel cuffs dragging across the table. "But it was that easy. We would listen on a four or five-minute conversation and figure out who was more likely involved in illegal activities. Once we figured out they were selling drugs, we would follow them. We were able to figure out where they stashed money and drugs. We knew who the high-priority couriers were, and who the wholesalers were."

Miller looked up, his pen pausing. "Did your unit execute the warrants on those stashes?"

"No," Hammon said, a dark smile touching his lips. "Rival drug dealers were blamed when we robbed them, because we drove vehicles similar to theirs. We used informants as lookouts just in case something went wrong. If the targets started changing their operational security, the sky grid adjusted instantly. Suspects would switch cell phones, and we would fly over them and get the new cell phone number as soon as they leave the wireless company. We paid associates at the phone company to give us the phone numbers of customers who we thought were into illegal activity."

Hammon's eyes drifted toward the two-way mirror. "But the leak didn't just flow one way. Every time we talked to a witness, they would find out within minutes. They knew the whole conversation and the agents involved. At times, I feared for my life. I found myself looking over my shoulder almost every day."

The aviation grid had become a multi-million-dollar obsession, a closed loop of constant flight paths that produced absolutely nothing.

"We were stuck in planes for up to eight hours a day, every day for years," Hammon murmured, his voice heavy with the memory of the cramped cabins. "

We hadn't got anywhere in the years following this suspect. All we knew is him and his guys hated a dirty cop; we just couldn't figure out the dirty cop.

CHAPTER FIVE

Once we got a clue on who the dirty cop was, we would intercept another conversation pointing to another cop. As frustrating as it was, we never gave up and continued our aerial surveillance."

The lead investigator leaned over his file. "Is that when the parameters of the operation changed?"

"As time went on," Hammon stated, his tone turning deadly serious, "one of the agents said we should just kill him. I knew they were not on the up and up, but I didn't expect murdering someone. As soon as my shift was over, I told my superior. He informed me to go along with it for the time being."

Miller's hand shook slightly as he recorded the words. "They were planning an extrajudicial execution?"

"They were contemplating killing a man who they suspected was dealing drugs, and couldn't catch him," Hammon confirmed. "We had no proof he was a drug dealer—just a rumor. Word on the street is he had millions of dollars, but no one knew where it was."

The tactical logs from that specific tracking window detailed the exact moment the field unit realized they were chasing a shadow.

"Suspect is going in the store," the ground tail reported from an unmarked sedan.

The airborne analyst pinned the location on his digital map. "Copy that. Keep visual on the exit."

An hour passed in complete silence. The heat signatures inside the commercial structure shifted and blurred.

"He's been in there for an hour," the ground agent radioed, his tone tight with frustration. "I'm going in."

The channel stayed silent for three minutes before the agent's voice cut through, sounding entirely bewildered. "He's not in here. He's gone."

Back in the command center, the supervisor slammed his headset onto the desk. "It's looking more and more like someone in law enforcement has a hand in this cover-up. How do they know our every move?"

"I have to assume my house is bugged," the secondary analyst muttered, staring at his monitor.

"How else would they know who the informants are?"

"I think you're right," the supervisor sighed. "Either they are speaking in code, or we have a problem with corruption."

"I think they are speaking in code," the analyst countered, trying to maintain his composure. "We have too many good agents who will die for the people of this country."

The supervisor rubbed his eyes, looking up at the flight tracking boards. "You never truly know a person's heart. That being said, we should focus more on the wiretaps."

The lead investigator turned his attention back to the former agent, pushing the tape recorder closer to the center of the table.

"Agent Hammon, what type of an advantage do you have from the sky?"

"We can see how people move about an entire city," Hammon answered cleanly.

"Were IMSI catchers on those aerial vehicles?"

"Yes."

"What was the reason for having so many planes and drones in the air at one time?" the lead investigator asked.

"We have a high-priority target we can't let out of our sight," Hammon stated.

"Is this the same target that was being entrapped?" Miller asked.

"Yes."

The lead investigator tapped his pen against the affidavit. "Approximately how many planes and drones were in the sky at one time?"

"During the day, ten to twelve planes and three or four drones," Hammon recited from memory. "At night, twenty to thirty planes and up to sixty drones."

Miller looked up, astounded by the scale. "Who controlled each drone?" "One operator can control fifteen to twenty drones at one time," Hammon explained. "The software handles the flight stability; the operator just tracks the intelligence vectors."

The lead investigator leaned forward, his voice dropping into a careful register. "I'm aware that some of this information is classified and will be heard in a courtroom, but can you tell us if you could hear a target's phone conversation in real time from the planes?"

"Yes," Hammon said flatly.

"Can you elaborate?"

"I can't," Hammon replied, his eyes dropping to his chained wrists.

The lead investigator didn't push the classified boundary, shifting his question slightly. "How did you know a target would be at a certain location?"

"We have algorithm prediction software," Hammon revealed.

"Has this software been wrong?" Miller asked.

"Yes," Hammon said, his voice echoing in the quiet room. "But after we follow a target for a while, patterns get developed. The software learns where they sleep, where they eat, and who they trust. It turns a human life into an equation."

The surveillance apparatus of Americana extended its reaching fingers right into the neon-lit corridors of the entertainment

districts. The state's methods of physical entry had adapted, utilizing the hospitality industry as a legal shield.

Casinos were working with federal authorities, giving informants lines of credit in order to play at tables. The high-roller invites and free chips weren't perks; they were tactical anchors designed to keep a target stationary. While suspects were gambling in the casinos, drug agents were in their hotel rooms searching without a warrant.

It was a clean, quiet trespass masked by the ringing of slot machines and the shuffling of cards stories below.

But the silence of the operation shattered instantly when a local police frequency exploded with a priority-one dispatch.

“Breaking news,” the 12 News Network emergency broadcast alert popped up on John's monitor. “Another dirty cop gunned down while sitting in his patrol car with his mistress.”

John rubbed his face, staring at the flashing red text on his screen. “This is getting ridiculous.”

“All of these honest cops have mistresses,” his desk editor muttered sarcastically, tossing a fresh incident report onto the desk. “Every case he handled should be looked at. The integrity of his entire arrest history is completely compromised.”

“They killed him and the woman?” John asked, scanning the bullet-hole trajectory mapping.

“Yes.”

“They will sweep it under the rug, and eventually it will go away,” John stated flatly, his voice hollow with institutional exhaustion. “You’re right. They would never investigate one of their own for corruption, unless the public finds out first.”

The editor leaned over the glass partition. “How do you think the wives feel finding out their spouse was killed, but also having an affair?”

John didn't look up from his typing. “They have a pension for life. They don’t feel anything.”Inside the monitoring post, a technician pressed his headset tightly against his ear. “Call coming in.”

The audio signal from the casino wire stabilized, revealing a heated conversation between two mid-level handlers regarding their street-level resources.

"I can't understand how this person is a known extortionist and drug dealer, and the government uses him as an informant," the first handler grumbled over the line.

"Meet me at the casino," the director ordered curtly, cutting off the complaint. "We need eyes on the floor now."

The narrative cuts abruptly to a luxury suite on the twenty-second floor of the resort complex, where a local vice squad had executed a separate, unauthorized sweep based on a local tip.

"Vice is here to search the room," a local detective radioed back to his precinct dispatcher. He kicked open a locked closet door, exposing a massive, military-grade duffel bag packed to the brim with tightly bound stacks of currency. He whistled sharply. "Call the FBS. This is a lot of cash."

The precinct captain arrived on scene twenty minutes later, his face pale as he reviewed the registration data on the room's television monitor. "The room is registered to an undercover drug agent."

The panic was immediate. The captain grabbed the lead vice detective by the collar, pulling him away from the cash. "Do whatever you have to do to stop this from being made public."

"Why would a drug agent be running a sting alone?" the detective questioned, refusing to let go of the file.

"I think we have a dirty cop on our hands," the captain whispered tightly. "Can you pull up the video when they checked in?

Trace his phone, and find out who he was talking to when he pulled up."

The wiretap net didn't just capture high-level drug drops; it sifted through the casual domestic conversations of the entire city, fishing for any thread that could be used as social or financial leverage.

"We picked up on a call where a dentist is telling his wife he suspects that a local police officer is beating his wife, and knocked her teeth out," an analyst reported to his shift supervisor.

The supervisor didn't look up from his ledger. "Can you find out who the cop is?"

"Working on it," the analyst replied, typing a fresh query into the department personnel database. "The only problem is she admitted it was a car wreck. She's already locked into the official accident report. If we squeeze her to change her story, we threaten her with filing a false police report charge."

The analyst paused, his eyes widening as a separate notification flashed on his terminal screen.

"Look at the news. There is a video showing drug agents' training techniques."

The supervisor spun around in his chair. "Someone recorded an undercover video showing drug agent training?"

"Yes," the analyst confirmed, clicking on a leaking social media link.

The raw footage displayed a stark, unedited tactical gym. An instructor wearing an official tactical vest was demonstrating field compliance tactics on a dummy asset. The officer in the video was screaming, *"Stop reaching for my gun!"* when clearly the guy isn't moving. It was a premeditated lesson in manufacturing a lethal threat for the body cameras.

"How are they getting all these videos?" the supervisor barked, slamming his hand onto the desk.

"Someone has been releasing videos every four days of cops committing crimes," the analyst stated grimly. "The reverse leak is automated. It's a scheduled distribution."

The supervisor's jaw tightened.

"Keep listening to the calls, and if you find anything interesting, check for felonies or warrants. We need counter-leverage before the morning cycle."

John sat in the primary editing studio of 12 News Network, finalizing the graphics layout for the upcoming evening broadcast. The network promo was already running on the lower tickers.

"12 News Network is doing a piece on IMSI catchers tomorrow night," John told his chief technician.

The technician laughed, uploading the signal-theft maps. "Civil rights lawyers are going to have a field day with this one. The signal dumps are entirely unconstitutional."

Back in the federal tracking room, a sudden data spike triggered a high-priority alert across the casino sector monitors.

"We have something!" the monitor analyst shouted.

"There is a guy who sounds pretty pissed about being followed by undercover agents."

The supervisor rushed to the console. "Is he in the casino at this time?"

"Yes."

"Get some people in his room now," the supervisor ordered. "Catch him before he clears the floor."

The tracking van's GPS coordinates updated in real time, but the target was moving faster than the physical teams could deploy.

"He's leaving the property," the ground unit reported, watching a black sedan blow past the valet gate. "He's going to a private airstrip."

The supervisor checked the resort's digital registry system. "Did he check out?"

"No."

"Someone is helping him, and he knows he's being recorded," the supervisor stated, his voice heavy with the realization that the inner loop had failed entirely.

The structural collapse of the agency's mission was total. John's voiceover for the investigative piece played through the studio monitors, sealing the final page of the broadcast report:

"The DEA efficiency rate is less than 1% in stopping the flow of illegal narcotics into Union South. It's a failed mission."

Inside the windowless tracking hub, the supervisor rubbed his temples as the latest data sheets flatlined on the screen. The financial expense of keeping the planes in the sky was mounting, yet the database remained empty of any actionable intelligence.

"No crimes until we started sending people his way, it isn't right," Miller muttered, leaning over his terminal. He looked across at his partner, the moral weight of the multi-year dragnet finally showing in his slumped shoulders.

"Hey, he used to be a criminal," the supervisor shot back, his voice hardening defensively. "Regardless if he's changed or not, what did he get away with in the past? The system demands a return on investment."

An analyst tapped his headset sharply, cutting off the argument. "He's getting a call now."

The waveform on the center monitor split as the intercept software bypassed the target's encryption.

"So, as long as they get the conviction, they'll do anything to not expose states' secrets?" the target's voice crackled through the speakers, talking to an unknown legal advisor on a secure frequency.

"That's how it works!" the advisor replied bitterly. "The State Secrets Act is their ultimate shield. They'll drop an entire indictment before they let a defense attorney audit their digital infrastructure."

Miller stared at the text transcript scrolling down his screen. "We've been following him for years, and he's clean."

"It doesn't matter," the supervisor snapped. He snatched the desk phone, dialing an internal, direct line extension to the federal building.

The line rang once before a sharp voice answered. "Hello."

"Union South Attorney's office," the supervisor identified himself quickly. "I have an informant that can tell you everything. Can you give him a deal?"

The prosecutor on the other end didn't hesitate. "Bring him in now."

"You got it," the supervisor said, slamming the receiver back down onto its cradle.

Miller watched his boss walk out of the room, turning his head toward the junior analyst. "Why would a prosecutor be nervous, unless he's guilty of something?"

The analyst shrugged, keeping his eyes on the live terminal. "My thoughts exactly."

Deep within the centralized logistics center of the Union South task force, the administrative lines handled hundreds of anonymous communications daily. The desk officer answered a blinking line on the secure console.

"Tips line," the officer stated automatically.

"Can I get a reward for turning in dirty cops?" a distorted, low voice questioned on the other end.

The officer adjusted his recorder. "We pay rewards for crimes being committed or are about to be committed."

"I want to talk to someone that is in charge of Operation Black Phantom," the caller demanded flatly.

The officer's fingers froze over his keyboard. *Black Phantom* was a highly classified internal tracking protocol, completely hidden from public files. He immediately hit the transfer toggle. "Hold please."

He switched to the commander's private line. "We have a potential informant asking about Black Phantom."

The commander picked up instantly. "Hello. Sir, what's your name?"

"I want to talk about the reward before I tell you anything," the caller countered, entirely unfazed by the commander's authoritative tone.

"The rewards start at $10k for credible information leading to a conviction," the commander stated, trying to establish a baseline.

"OK," the caller murmured. "Word on the street is you guys want to know who Big Dog is, correct?"

The commander leaned forward, his heart hammering against his ribs. *Big Dog* was the unverified codename of the leak inside the department. "Yes."

"Big Dog is a federal agent," the informant revealed, a grim certainty in his voice. "That's how they know your every move."

The commander gripped the edge of his desk. "What's his real name?"

"Until I have a reward, I can't tell you anything," the caller said. "Cash only."

"We can't give you cash," the commander countered. "Federal disbursements require a signed voucher and a bank wire."

"$50k cash," the informant demanded, ignoring the protocol. "I want to be able to relocate my family and start fresh."

"It's not going to happen," the commander refused. "The accounting trail is absolute."

"You have until Monday at 4pm," the caller stated coldly. "If not, I'll never call back."

The line went completely dead. The commander stared at the flashing red disconnect light. "Ok, let me see..."

Outside the federal buildings, John stood on the roof of the 12 News Network parking garage, watching the evening sky deepen into a dark purple. Beside him, an independent network technician adjusted a wide-band signal antenna.

John pointed upward toward a faint, moving light blinking just beneath the cloud line. "Look in the sky. Those aren't stars. Those are surveillance drones equipped with IMSI catchers."

"The legal defense teams are starting to catch on," the technician noted, looking down at his laptop diagnostics. "I was reading the latest defense briefs from the courthouse. The attorneys are filing constitutional mandates. One text read: *'I have the fundamental right to confront my accuser.'* But how do you cross-examine an algorithm?"

The tracking team, however, was already exploiting the very legal communications meant to protect the targets. Back in the intercept van, an analyst pushed a printed page toward the supervisor.

"We picked up on a call from a defendant to his lawyer," the analyst reported. "They are planning for a trial."

The supervisor scanned the defense strategy notes with a cold expression. "Print the transcript and give it to the Union South attorney. Give them the entire layout of the defense cross-examination before they walk into the room."

"Just do what you can," the analyst murmured, turning back to his board. "I have a feeling there are more dirty prosecutors than we think."

"I think they are pulling the strings," the supervisor admitted flatly. "There is no way a federal judge will go against a federal prosecutor. The institutional bond is too tight."

John's investigation at the news network was zeroing in on that exact structural trap. He met his chief researcher in the archive room, surrounded by old court dockets.

"We have to prove that they entrapped these individuals, including my client," John said, pinning a list of fabricated stings to the wall.

"The nation is on high alert right now. Look at any recently released federal prisoners who claimed to have been framed. If the stories match, we have our pattern."

The researcher flipped through a stack of active federal warrants. "We have someone who fits that description, and he skipped out on federal parole."

John's eyes narrowed. "Find him."

"Everyone we've talked to says he's at the casino," the researcher revealed.

John reached for his coat. "Do whatever it takes. We can't have the American citizens losing trust in law enforcement. Once that trust breaks down entirely, the whole facade crumbles."

The internal collapse of the agency reached its apex when the Federal Bureau of Security officially crossed lines with the narcotics task force.

Inside the gray interrogation cell, the lead investigator slid a fresh, unredacted deconfliction log across the metal table toward the former agent.

"FBS has opened an investigation into Agent Hammon," the investigator stated plainly, the recording spools capturing the words. "They think Agent Hammon is a corrupt DEA agent."

"FBS has opened an investigation into Agent Hammon," the investigator stated plainly, the recording spools capturing the words. "They think Agent Hammon is a corrupt DEA agent."

Hammon looked down at the file, his expression unchanging.

"He comes up in the deconfliction database. I think the Federal Government is investigating him also. The right hand doesn't know what the left hand is cutting deals with."

The investigator leaned back, his tone turning cynical. "I wouldn't put much trust in the DEA. They've been orchestrating a failed mission for decades."

Miller blinked, looking up from his notes. "That's a little harsh, don't you think?"

"Anytime your efficiency rate is 1% in stopping the flow of narcotics, your mission is a failure, wouldn't you agree?"

Hammon countered smoothly, looking directly at the investigator.

The investigator didn't dispute the statistic, shifting his focus straight down to the physical mechanics of the data extractions executed by Hammon's old field unit.

"Agent Hammon, did you or any other agent trade cell phone chargers with any targets?" the investigator demanded.

"Yes," Hammon admitted without a shred of hesitation.

Miller leaned forward, his pen poised. "Why?"

"We needed to download the contents of the target's phone," Hammon explained, his voice dropping into a chillingly practical register. "The charger wasn't just a power supply; it was hardwired with a forensic extraction chip.

The moment they plugged their device in to get a charge, the software copied the entire operating system—contacts, photos, encrypted keys—and transmitted it back to our surveillance van via a local wireless bridge."

The lead investigator clicked his pen against the cold table, his eyes locked onto Hammon's. "Did you have a warrant?"

The counter-investigation unfolding outside the courthouse was outstripping the official dockets. In his private brick office two blocks from the city square, the senior defense attorney threw a packet of unredacted photographs onto the table.

"One of my clients sent me a picture of a listening device in his wall plug," the attorney stated, his voice flat with clinical rage. He looked across at his chief investigator. "If they aren't sending silent texts to my clients in order to install malware on their phones, they are placing listening devices in their homes."

The investigator sighed, leaning against the heavy mahogany desk. "The local tactical units are claiming the intercepts are necessary for officer safety. They're complaining about the hostile climate on the streets."

The attorney let out a cold, sharp laugh. "I'm a defense attorney, I chose this career. When I hear a police officer cry about being targeted and shot at, I don't feel bad for them—quit. No one is making you do this job, find something less stressful or stop complaining."

He pulled a fresh copy of the federal motion from his brief case.

"This prosecutor is very vindictive, therefore make sure to check

and double-check everything you do. The government has the resources to put surveillance on you twenty-four hours a day. If they can't get you with all the charges, they will split them with the state, and they both will have a crack at prosecuting you ."

The investigator checked the judge's recent docket history.

"Your other problem is this judge agreed to all the wiretaps and

warrants, so he might think there is some wrongdoing going on."

"As a defense attorney, my job is to protect my client," the lawyer countered, tightening his jaw. "You can't do that with a dirty judge ."

"Can we get him removed?" the investigator asked.

"I'm not sure you want to try," the attorney admitted honestly. "If it doesn't work, you're in front of a judge you tried to have removed. If I don't try, my client will be found guilty, and I will be obligated to file an appeal."

During this time, investigators were investigating prosecutors and judges. Grand juries were compromised, and the investigation they did was to shut the public up. The architecture of the oversight was a total theater.

The deeper the research cut, the clearer the institutional paralysis became. Could the system be corrupt?

"One would think the judicial system is full of honest individuals, but that's not the case," the attorney murmured, staring out the window at the flashing blue lights of a routine traffic stop below. "Every day you hear about a cop who was law enforcement of the year, arrested for beating his wife, killing an unarmed suspect, planting drugs, or lying to a grand jury."

He shook his head, pointing to an active use-of-force file. "I can't understand how someone running away from you can be a threat. I've defended many men, and they all say the same thing: if they stay, they will get beat or killed, so they run and still get beat or killed ."

"It's the society we live in," the investigator said grimly. "There's nothing we can do until qualified immunity is removed."

"That's going to take the Supreme Court, and that will never happen," the attorney stated flatly. "You have members of the Supreme Court that say if a cop didn't know he was doing wrong by planting evidence, he's not guilty—but if I plant something on someone, I'm going to prison. The police unions have powerful lobbyists that most civilians can't fight."

The lawyer sat back down, sliding a blank check across the wood. "Bring in a private investigator, and see what we can find out about some of these elected officials."

"You need to be careful," the investigator warned, refusing to touch the paper. "They can do things to you that you wouldn't imagine. If they kidnap protesters in broad daylight and torture them for information, imagine what they will do to a lawyer that will expose them."

The attorney's eyes narrowed into sharp slits. "That's it. If I can get them to harass me, and I can get proof of what they do to whistleblowers, I will have proof the government is hiding corruption. I'm more afraid of the lawyers; they are more ruthless than the hardened criminals I've represented for more than thirty years."

"What if we could get the cops to carry liability insurance?" the investigator suggested.

"It will never happen, the union will step in," the lawyer dismissed instantly. "Sooner or later, a bad cop will be placed at a police station in another city, and they will have no clue of what he did here. Our citizens will have to take things into their own hands."

The investigator tilted his head. "What do you mean?"

The lawyer leaned across the layout, his plan completely shifting the parameters of the struggle.

"Record the police," the attorney ordered. "Take shifts and record every hour of their workday."

"Is that legal?" the investigator asked.

"They are government employees; we can record them as long as they are at work on the taxpayers' dollar. Some steal time while working for the city, others are on lunch with their mistresses, and the public should know this. How can you be a trustworthy individual and you have a mistress?

Your wife should know. You can't collect a private check while also collecting taxpayers' money."

He pulled up a map of the precinct limits. "There are 113 sworn officers, and there are three shifts; we need to get cameras rolling on every inch of this city twenty-four hours a day, seven days a week. We want to investigate them how they investigate us—make them feel uncomfortable."

"I think they will try and charge us with stalking," the investigator cautioned.

"As long as you are in public, you have no expectations of privacy," the lawyer countered. "That is true. We don't have to worry about anything; we aren't doing anything wrong. Like they tell us, if you don't have nothing to hide, why don't you want to be recorded? Every morning I want to wake up, and a dirty cop is charged with a crime. Hold them accountable, and we will see change in this country."

He tapped the table for emphasis. "Until they turn on the dirty cops, record them. Eventually, they will grow tired of being under surveillance. FOIA any jobs they have outside of the government, and see if they are stealing time."

"I doubt very seriously if the government will give us information to convict one of their own," the investigator muttered.

"You're right," the lawyer agreed smoothly. "But all we want is for them to deny us access and keep a record of them doing it. The cover-up is worse than the crime, always remember that. I know things they have no idea I'm aware of."

The attorney stopped, his eyes dropping to the investigator's coat pocket. "Do you have a phone on you?"

"Yes, why?"

"I told you plenty of times that they can turn on your camera and your microphone on your phone," the lawyer warned sharply.

"It's off," the investigator replied.

"Regardless if it's off or not, they can turn it on," the attorney stated flatly. "Consider the drones in the sky at night—some are manned, some are not. What do you mean? They have unmanned drones that are equipped with cameras, and they can see everything you do. What about the infrared cameras that can see inside your house? They have to have strong evidence to use those, but I wouldn't put anything past the USSA."

The investigator shook his head, looking at the logistical lists. "How are we going to convince hundreds of people to follow these cops?"

The lawyer's expression turned entirely unyielding. "Do what cops do and lie; make up stories about suspects no matter how bad. It just baffles me that dirty cops have to entrap criminals—if someone is committing crimes, why would you have to set them up?"

"Exactly," the investigator whispered.

CHAPTER SIX

On the commercial strip of the western sector, an unmarked sedan pulled sharply into the gravel lot of a local fleet transit office. Two field agents wearing heavy dark coats stepped out, walking directly into the glass lobby.

They approached the front counter where the business owner sat logging vehicle returns.

"We are here from the FBS," the lead agent announced, flashing a dark leather credentials case.The owner didn't look up from his ledger. "Okay, how can I help you?"

"We would like to know who rented this car last," the agent stated, pointing a finger through the window toward a gray sedan parked in the bay.

The owner shut his log book with a heavy thud. "We don't give information about our customers without a warrant."

The agent's face tightened, his eyes narrowing.

"Okay, we'll get a warrant."

"Go get it then," the owner replied, completely unfazed.

The secondary agent let out a dry, cynical laugh, crossing his arms. "It's strange a business owner doesn't want to help the police."

"I know, right," the owner countered, looking both agents dead in the eye. "Maybe we've been watching the news and see how you frame and beat individuals."

The lead agent stepped closer to the counter, his posture turning rigid. "That's a narrative the news puts out to discredit law enforcement."

The owner didn't flinch. "So, why are police being arrested or investigated every day for corruption?"

The lead agent's fingers twitched near his coat pocket, his face hardening as he stared at the rental desk counter. He didn't move. He expected the flashing of a gold badge to clear any administrative hurdle in Americana, but the wall before him remained entirely unyielding.

"Go get your warrant," the owner stated, his voice flat, dropping his pen onto the open ledger. "Don't come back until you do."

The agents swapped a tight, infuriated look before turning on their heels, their heavy boots scuffing the linoleum as they kicked the glass door open and stepped out into the humid midday heat. Inside the lobby, the rental clerk let out a long, shaky breath, leaning his hands heavily against the counter.

"Can you believe this?" the clerk whispered, watching the unmarked sedan pull out of the gravel lot. "They just walk in like they own the place because they flash a badge."

The owner picked up his pen, his expression carved from stone. "Your badge is not what it once meant. No one respects you guys anymore."

He walked to the window, watching the dust settle by the curb.

The division between the precinct houses and the neighborhoods of Americana had turned from a line in the sand into an open canyon. The trust was gone, evaporated by decades of wiretaps, roadside thefts, and unconstitutional data sweeps.

Two blocks away, at a community outreach meeting inside a local recreation center, a regional director stood behind a wooden podium, addressing a sparse, hostile crowd of local business operators.

"We are here to gain the community's trust," the director announced, his hands spread wide in a practiced gesture of transparency.

A mechanic in grease-stained coveralls stood up from the back row, his voice echoing sharply off the gymnasium walls. "Start with investigating these dirty cops."

The director adjusted his glasses, his posture turning instantly defensive. "We can't investigate if you won't tell us."

"You do your own job," the mechanic shot back, refusing to sit down.

"We can't get the bad cops off the streets if the people don't tell us," the director argued, his tone picking up a patronizing edge.

The mechanic let out a harsh, mocking laugh. "I've seen what has happened to cops who turned on their own, so no thank you.

These pieces of shit are on video choking other cops and nothing happens—that tells me I have no chance as a regular civilian. If the blue line protects a monster who attacks another uniform, what do you think they'll do to me?"

The director cleared his throat, shifting his paperwork nervously. "Send me in the direction I need to investigate."

The mechanic pointed a calloused finger directly at the stage. "Start with overtime and extra jobs. You can't work for the city and private companies at the same time and get paid for both.

Check the log sheets against the private security payrolls. The numbers don't lie."

He turned, grabbing his jacket from the back of his chair. "Good day, gentlemen."

Deep within the centralized tracking station, the audio monitors hummed with the steady, overlapping frequencies of the city's cellular grid. A senior analyst adjusted the equalization settings on his console, dragging a fresh, flagged digital capture into the primary analysis software.

"We have a new case we need to look at," the analyst reported, signaling his shift supervisor over.

The supervisor leaned over the high-definition monitor. "What is it?"

"One of our informants is playing both sides," the analyst revealed, pointing to a recurring voice print match on a non-secure line.

The supervisor's jaw tightened. "How do you know this?"

"One of the calls we are monitoring spoke about an informant who feels guilty about setting people up," the analyst explained, scrolling through the automated text transcript. "He's talking to an outside source, spilling the parameters of the stings we've been running out of the car customization shop."

The supervisor let out a long, low sigh, staring at the pulsing audio waves. "This is a problem."

"You're right about that," the analyst muttered. He hit a separate macro key, pulling up a live local news feed on the secondary monitor. "On top of that, another death from a no-knock warrant just hit the wires in the western sector."

The supervisor watched the raw, shaky cell phone footage of a neighborhood in chaos, flashing police lights illuminating a broken front door. "Hate to say it, but he was right. The people have lost trust in law enforcement. The tactics are tearing the system apart faster than we can clean up the files."

The media side of the struggle was hitting the same institutional brick walls. Inside the 12 News Network studio, John sat at his workstation, staring at a massive, encrypted PDF file that had arrived through a secure, anonymous dead-drop server.

His lead researcher stepped into the room, closing the door behind her. "I received an anonymous email with the personnel file of federal agents."

John zoomed in on the document's metadata. "Who do you think it was from?"

"I think it's someone in law enforcement who is afraid to expose corruption," the researcher stated, pulling up a chair. "Someone inside the complex who couldn't stand the Canal Street cover-up anymore."

John scrolled down the endless pages, his eyes narrowing as he saw the heavy bars of solid black ink obscuring nearly every line of text. "What is in it?"

"Hundreds of pages of complaints," the researcher said, her voice tight with frustration. "Mostly redacted."

John tapped the screen. "Why would the personnel file be redacted to this extent?"

"Because if the Union South Department of Justice comes in and does an investigation, the names of the witnesses are removed and you can't question them," the researcher explained. "It's a protective loop.

They claim privacy laws, but it's designed to kill the trail. Some of these agents have ten or fifteen complaints logged against them for predatory behavior, use of force, and evidence tampering."

John leaned back in his chair, shaking his head. "I have no idea how they are members of law enforcement with this predatory behavior. No wonder citizens run when the police pull them over—they fear for their lives."

The researcher shook her head, trying to maintain her professional distance. "You are over-exaggerating, John. It's a systemic filing issue, not a street-level directive."

"If we don't have the victims' names, we will never know what happened," John pushed, ignoring the dismissal. "The files are useless without the identities of the people they squeezed."

"Try looking at complaint boards and see who is complaining about cops," the researcher suggested, pointing to a list of independent public forums.

John let out a dry, hollow laugh. "That's easier said than done. The government will just put in for a warrant and see who is looking up complaints made about cops. They monitor the IP traffic on those server domains. If not, they will do a tower dump over the area to harvest the MAC addresses of any device accessing the site."

He scrolled down further, stopping at a specific, less-redacted internal memo from a regional administrative unit.

"From what I've read here, women are complaining about being harassed inside the division office," John muttered, reading the raw text beneath the black bars. "This predator is sticking his hands up the dresses of the women he manages. One woman said he wouldn't stop rubbing up against her in the break room."

The researcher's expression turned cold as she read over his shoulder. "And these are the men we should trust in the community."

"Not just men," John noted, his finger tracing a line on the next page. "There is a woman who witnessed it and turned her head.

At no time did she try to reach out to this woman and console her."

The researcher turned toward the door, her jaw set. "That's the thin line. The culture demands compliance above everything else, even basic human decency."

John closed the file and looked up. "Can you give me a background check on this prosecutor? The one handling the customization shop cases."

"Sure," the researcher said, her hand on the doorknob. "What do you need to know?"

"Everything you can find out. Financials, properties, campaign donors, former cases. Everything."

"You got it."

The tracking van parked around the corner from John's residential street sat in complete darkness, its engine idling silently to power the surveillance racks inside. From his front porch, John could see the dull metallic gleam of the roof antennas through the low cypress branches.

He held his encrypted satellite phone to his ear, listening to the gravelly voice of his contact inside the federal complex.

"The FBS is parked around the corner of my house in a van," John stated, his voice flat.

"Don't worry," the contact replied through the static. "They are just doing surveillance and stealing your data. They want to see who walks through your front door. Let me ask you—during the deposition, did you allow the government to download your phone contents?"

"I never brought a phone in," John said.

"Good. If you had it on you, they would have harvested the firmware via the local terminal. They are going to try and intimidate you, John. Be prepared."

“It has already started,” John murmured, looking down at his keys. “They follow me every morning when I pull out of the driveway. Two vehicles, rotating at the intersections.”

“As long as you aren’t doing anything wrong, you don’t have anything to worry about from a legal standpoint,” the contact said, though his tone carried an underlying warning.

“But watch the physical interactions.”

John walked back into his kitchen, leaning against the counter. “I have had individuals come up to me at gas stations trying to sell me electronics. IPads, high-end cameras, car audio gear. It’s happened three times this week.”

“That’s one of the things they do,” the contact explained cleanly. “It’s a classic street ambush. If you buy it, the government already has the serial numbers in a database as stolen, and you will be charged with that crime instantly. They use fake fencing operations to manufacture a felony when they can't find a real one.”

“Is there anything I can do?” John asked, his hand tightening on the receiver.

“You can’t do anything! As long as they think you are, or are about to commit a crime, they can investigate you. The statutory definition of 'suspicion' is entirely elastic.”

“What about counter-surveillance?”

“You can video anything you see in public,” the contact encouraged sharply. “I actually encourage you to document strange men following you and trying to hold conversations with you. Record the faces, record the plates. Build your own database.”

John looked out his window at the empty street. "Some of my closest friends have distanced themselves from me. People I've known for ten years won't return a text."

"The goal of the government is to leave you stuck by yourself with no help," the contact stated flatly. "They isolate the target until the psychological pressure forces a collapse. They make up lies, and the court allows it."

"This doesn't seem right," John whispered.

"Members of law enforcement can lie to anyone at any time to further an investigation, even when it can cause physical and financial harm to innocent people. The supreme courts have ruled that deception is a legitimate tool of the state."

"It just doesn't sit well with me," John said, looking at his notes on the counter. "That they can roam the streets of this community, lie to the citizens, and destroy innocent lives."

The contact let out a short, cynical breath. "Only in Union South, land of the free."

"Right," John replied. "Can we get someone inside the complex to document what's going on? Someone with access to the server logs?"

"I can check and see," the contact murmured, his voice dropping lower. "But you have to be prepared for the worst-case scenario, John. If they pull you in on an administrative hold, they will try to feed you spoiled and rotten food. They may put glass, feces, and rat poison in your food inside the holding cells to break your health. They can lock you in solitary confinement for years to silence you before a trial even begins."

John took a deep breath, his eyes hardening. "Our goal is to gather as much evidence as possible, so when they say they have completed their investigation and continue to say they found no wrongdoing, we can come in and prove they lied."

"They won't just confess, John," the contact warned. "They will just move the goalpost and say they were trying to confuse the bad actors by saying they've completed the investigation. It's an infinite shell game. We can show numerous fake articles orchestrated by law enforcement in the local papers. They call it *tickling the wires*—where they leak stories that aren't true to the media just to get suspects to talk about crimes on the wiretaps."

John looked down at his terminal, where a fresh court notification had just popped up. He clicked it open, his face falling.

"They have already dismissed all the cases against all of the officers," John said, staring at the electronic signature of the federal judge. "The Canal Street raid, the evidence thefts... it's all gone. Wiped clean from the docket."

"The credibility of these officers should be called into question," the contact muttered over the line.

John closed the browser tab, his expression entirely grim. "It will never happen."

The heavy mahogany desk in the defense attorney's war room was buried under emergency motions, half-redacted court dockets, and encrypted data logs. The air-conditioning unit vibrated against the brick wall, a low, mechanical hum that offered no relief from the building pressure.

"You have to think outside the box," the senior attorney barked, slamming his fist onto a stack of federal appeals briefs. He locked eyes with his lead investigator, his expression entirely fierce. "They are going to bring the weight of the U.S. Government down on us, and we need to be prepared."

The investigator rubbed his bloodshot eyes, staring out the window at the gray skyline of Americana. "Well, they have an advantage from the sky we will never get. The drone patterns changed again this morning. They're running tighter vectors over the neighborhood grid."

The office door opened, and the junior partner stepped in, his face tight and pale. He tossed a certified court delivery packet onto the desk. "By the way, the government has requested all correspondence be declined."

The senior attorney snapped his head up. "They are denying writing material for my client?"

"Yes," the partner confirmed quietly. "Total administrative isolation. No legal pads, no pens, no incoming mail. They're locking him down to break his focus before the suppression hearing."

The senior attorney let out a harsh, bitter breath, leaning back in his chair. "There is a good chance the government has figured out who the mole is. They're cutting off the valves. If Hammon's pipeline to the press goes dark, they can bury the original analog tapes before a jury ever smells the frame-up."

The institutional rot that Hammon had detailed inside the gray interrogation room had its genesis in a specific, hidden room at the training complex. On the desk monitor in John's newsroom, an unredacted audio file from a leaked training seminar began to play, the digital waveform pulsing in sharp, jagged spikes.

"Everything you've learned at the academy, get it out of your head," a veteran instructor's voice boomed through the studio speakers, cold and completely predatory. *"We are the FBS, the biggest government agency in the world. We are road pirates. We are here to collect money for the government."*

John leaned closer to the audio deck, adjusting the filter settings to catch the ambient murmurs of the recruits in the background.

"Work the streets," the instructor continued, the pacing of his words deliberate and transactional. *"Get in good with the snitches. Without them, we can't get close to the real criminals. Local P.D. look up to us. Build a relationship with them, and they will give you tips. Look out for counter-surveillance. Some of these guys have more money than they can count. Without hesitation, they will take your life and think nothing of it. Remember, you are your brother's keeper—protect one another like your life depends on it. Get out there and get us some money."*

John clicked the pause button, the audio wave freezing on the black screen. He turned to his broadcast editor, his jaw set. "That was a training tape from the FBS."

"The government's job is to take all ill-gotten gains," the editor muttered, reading through the civil forfeiture tracking sheets.

John stood up, pacing the length of the editing bay. "My job is to make them prove it is ill-gotten. How can you pull over my client and search him because a dog hit on a car? What happens when the dog is wrong? You take my client's property and make them prove how they got it. The burden of proof is totally inverted. Police have an incentive to pull over every suspicious person they see: money."

Without any real evidence, federal agents are able to get a warrant signed by a judge. In many cases, informants don't exist, and the federal government can still make a case on fabricated evidence.

The digital baseline is easily adjusted in the database to fit whatever narrative the prosecutor needs to clear the grand jury.

The defense attorney's personal log book recorded the absolute boundary he had drawn between his practice and the officers of the Americana judicial complex.

"Do not talk to the FBS without your attorney present," the lawyer wrote, his heavy fountain pen cutting deep into the paper. "The main thing is that I don't negotiate. I don't talk to my enemy. I have never thought of myself as an officer of the court. That title and what goes with it is a way to manipulate a lawyer so the judge can exercise control. The theater of the courtroom is designed to force compliance, but the constitution isn't a suggestion."

He looked up as John walked into the office, carrying a fresh batch of unredacted traffic stop statistics from the western highway corridors.

"How can any prosecutor with a good conscience prosecute innocent people?" John asked, throwing the data sheets onto the desk.

"Conscience doesn't fund the precinct budget," the attorney replied flatly. "Look at these seizure numbers. Not only do you have to hide your money from criminals, you need to hide it from members of law enforcement. Traffic stops have turned into robbery, planting of evidence, murder, or beatings. The threat of violence is anticipated whenever you are pulled over, regardless of the race of the cop. The color of the uniform is all that matters."

He scanned the transaction logs John had pulled from the commercial banks. "Going to the bank and pulling out your own money raises suspicion now. If a small business owner withdraws ten grand in physical currency to pay his suppliers, the automated system triggers a suspicious activity report that goes straight to the internet tracking team."

John pointed to a specific recurring name on the highway interdiction log. "Look at this. The people of this country are fed up. It's the usual suspect. Look—same Trooper."

"I wonder how much money doesn't make it back to the vault," the attorney murmured, tracing the trooper's arrest dates. "Being a cop is lucrative.

With overtime theft and pocketing cash seizures, you can retire at thirty instead of fifty. You buy a couple of rental properties with the untraceable cash, and you're set for life while the targets are sitting in a state facility."

"Motorists are scared to death to say no to a search because of what may happen," John said, his voice tightening. "Most individuals give up their liberties in order to get the traffic stop over as soon as possible. They'll sign the consent waiver just to make sure they don't end up face down on the asphalt."

As a business owner who carries large amounts of cash, you are extorted by the very people paid to protect you. No matter what you say, it is used against you, and now you have to prove you earned the money legally. The government's job is to convince jurors that you are a hardcore criminal with gang ties, and when they can't prove it, they just make it up."

The lawyer leaned over his terminal, pulling up a archived press conference clip from the Department of Justice media channel. On the screen, a clean-cut prosecutor stood before a wall of microphones, smiling broadly as he announced a sweeping racketeering indictment.

"Why is it when they get a conviction, they are proud to hold a press conference?" John muttered, watching the video. "But when the case comes back and they find out they convicted the wrong man, it's *'we have no comment*? The arrogance of the office is absolute."

"Innocent businessmen and women are being tortured in court because they can't prove where they made their money," the attorney stated, closing the video player. "Many mom-and-pop businesses rely on cash to pay their suppliers, so they don't put money in the bank. They don't have corporate accountants to build a paper fortress. Regardless if you're innocent or not, the government's job is to take as much money from citizens as possible. The government has a reason to steal from American Citizens."

He pulled up a regional budget allocation chart. "Money confiscated from traffic stops is used to fund overtime and equipment. Local police departments send money up to federal agencies, who send the money back down after taking their cut. It's a closed-loop federal laundering system. Forget the Fourth Amendment; treat all of Union South like the enemy."

John turned toward the window, looking up at the gray clouds where the low drone of an invisible rotor hummed. "Take away my liberty because I'm scared of my shadow. As a civil rights attorney, this angers me. We are going to look up and have no freedoms left."

"Don't worry," the lawyer said with heavy irony. "The FBS and USSA are fighting every day to make sure we are protected from ourselves. Everything they use in Baghdad, they will eventually use in Union South. Drones, IMSI catchers, and robots were all used against terrorists; now they're used on American citizens. If they tell you to get out of your car and you don't, they will just send a robot near your car and blow you up under the guise of an imminent threat baseline."

"I'm not sure the Union South people will put up with the way police in this country act for too much longer," John said, his eyes tracking a patrol cruiser turning the corner below.

"Protesting doesn't work," the attorney dismissed flatly. "The streets are monitored by facial recognition before the crowds even form. I get twenty to thirty calls a week from motorists who

say that the police took their money for no reason and didn't charge them with a crime. These people don't have the resources to fight back, and the precinct knows this. They target the people who can't afford a retainer."

The desk phone on the attorney's central console buzzed sharply, the incoming line routing from the public intake desk downstairs. He hit the speaker button.

"Hello," the lawyer stated.

"I'm looking for a lawyer," a strained, hesitant voice came through the small speaker.

"What you got?" the attorney asked, pulling a fresh legal pad forward.

"I was pulled over by the police, and they took $10k dollars from me," the caller explained, the background noise echoing with the sound of a roadside diner.

The attorney didn't sugarcoat the reality. "It will cost you that much to get it back. The legal fees and the forensic filing will eat up the entirety of the currency."

The caller didn't hesitate. "I understand that. I just don't want them to have it, and they will think twice about doing it to someone else."

A grim, genuine smile touched the attorney's lips. He gripped the receiver. "My kind of guy—thinking of others. I tell you what: meet me here at my office at nine in the morning."

"You got it," the voice replied, and the line went dead.

The lawyer looked across the table at John, his expression turning entirely determined. "Every week, civil rights are being stepped on by the same people who swore to uphold them."

At exactly nine o'clock the following morning, the office door clicked open. A middle-aged man wearing a plain flannel shirt stepped into the conference room, his hands shaking slightly as he took a seat across from the legal team.

"Good morning," the attorney welcomed him, sliding a cup of coffee across the wood. "Tell me what happened?"

"My wife and I were driving down U.S. 99 on the way to the casino when a Trooper came out of nowhere," the man explained, his eyes fixed on the blank legal pad.

The attorney leaned forward, his pen balanced over the paper. "Were you speeding?"

"No," the man stated firmly.

The attorney's eyes narrowed into sharp focus. "Then what?"

CHAPTER SEVEN

The political arena of Americana was not immune to the dragnet. In a secluded corner of a secure law firm overlooking the capital district, Bob, the senior defense attorney, sat across a glass table from a prominent federal lawmaker. The blinds were drawn tight, blocking out the glare of the noon sun.

"Congressman," Bob said, his voice dropping into a cautious register.

"Good morning, Bob," the lawmaker replied, leaning back in his leather chair with a casual smile. "I never thanked you for the contribution to the campaign."

Bob didn't smile back. He slid a thick, encrypted file across the glass. "I'm not here for that. Do you have a minute?"

The congressman's smile faded at the attorney's posture. "Sure, what's going on?"

"The FBS and USSA are tapping your phone, and they are trying to unseat you," Bob revealed flatly.

The lawmaker froze, his hand hovering over his coffee cup. "How do you know this?"

"One of my clients is under investigation, and he gave me a tape of one of the investigators bragging about it," Bob explained, gesturing to the file. "They aren't just monitoring your staff, Congressman. They're recording your personal lines."

The legislator's face paled. "Should I be worried?"

"I would stay off the phone if I were you," Bob advised grimly. "They sit and listen to phone conversations all day, every day, without a warrant. The statutory boundaries don't exist for them anymore. There are drones over your house as we speak, and they have infrared cameras watching you."

The congressman stood up, pacing to the window, his eyes searching the low cloud line. "I can try and find out who authorized it."

Bob let out a short, cynical breath. "The same rule you voted for is being used to track you and every American citizen. The emergency security amendments you signed off on last session gave them the skeleton key."

The lawmaker turned back around, his jaw tight. "Is there anything else I need to worry about?"

"Like I said, stay off the phone. They can drop your network and bring it down, and the IMSI catcher can connect to your phone," Bob warned, gathering his coat.

"The signal interception is automated. If you're within a mile of their mobile arrays, your data belongs to them."

The congressman nodded slowly, his expression turning entirely grim. "Thanks."

"I'll be in touch," Bob said, walking toward the exit. He turned to his lead investigator, who was waiting by the door. "Get in touch with the private investigator, and see if we can get a tail on some of these agents."

"Yes, sir," the investigator replied.

"Find out anything you can about them, and every member of their family, and get it to me in 24 hours."

"Yes, sir."

Bob walked out of the office building, his mind tracing the expanding perimeter of the tracking net. He turned to John, who was waiting for him by the parking garage elevator.

"We are in a police state," Bob murmured, his voice heavy with frustration. "There are people in this country locked up because of these laws, and states are now legalizing marijuana. What happens to those who are rotting away in federal holding facilities while the market turns a profit on the outside? We as a country are over-criminalizing marijuana, and the legacy of those old warrants is still crushing families."

"My job as a civil rights lawyer is getting harder and harder," Bob continued, stepping into the elevator.

"The clients are abused or starved in prison. Illegal search and seizure... it's taking a hold of

my mental stability. The sheer volume of institutional deception is suffocating."

John looked at the metrics on his tablet. "Look on the bright side—you have plenty of work. With all these cases, maybe we should hire some help. Get some more lawyers and a secretary in here."

"That sounds like a good idea," Bob agreed, his eyes hardening. "The more attention we bring to the situation, the more publicity to the firm. We have to find a way to get rid of qualified immunity. Without getting rid of it, we will go nowhere. The courts will continue to dismiss every civil suit before it hits a jury."

He leaned against the elevator wall.

"We will never find two cases just alike, so we need someone in law enforcement willing to inform on this corruption. The precedent requires an exact match to pierce the immunity shield. Federal prosecutors ambush defendants; we need to figure out a way to ambush their investigators."

"We did come across a retired federal agent who put in for retirement before an investigation was launched," John revealed, scrolling through his index of internal personnel files.

Bob's eyes narrowed into sharp slits. "Make his retirement uncomfortable. The public should know a dirty cop is being paid by tax dollars. If he's sitting on a government pension funded by the people he robbed, he shouldn't sleep easy."

"He has a good standing in the community," John cautioned. "It will be hard to flip public opinion."

"Has he been faithful to his wife?" Bob asked coldly. "I've found that they all have good standing in the community, and are liars and cheaters. The public persona is just a mask to hide the rot. I'll never forget the video of a so-called good cop stuffing his vest full of money on a traffic stop."

"Inadmissible and will be thrown out of court," John reminded

him quietly.

"Exactly," Bob spat. "These good cops have destroyed the credibility of my clients, saying they are pimps, drug dealers, and cartel assassins, while they carry out the exact same crimes with a government vehicle. You would think this stuff comes out of a movie. They throw it against the wall and see what sticks. Without a warrant to search my client's car, we should be able to file a motion and get his property back."

John shook his head. "The warrant could have come from the USSA court, which we have no access to. The docket is entirely classified."

"The Union South people should know if the government is doing illegal surveillance on the people," Bob stated flatly. "I advise my clients to not resist when their rights are being violated, and record it if they can. You want the altercation documented.

Not only that, you want to show that these dirty cops show a pattern of deception. I think they are clearly investigating you in order to rob you. They are going to stores and asking how you are paying for things, getting the serial numbers off your bills to see how much money you have. They can see no crime is being committed, yet they continue to stalk citizens to rob them. These are very dangerous cops. They are patrolling these highways to gather resources for the government."The narrative cuts back sharply to the gray, sterile confines of the capital interrogation complex, where the recording wheels captured the final baseline of Agent Hammon's official statement.

"Agent Hammon, we appreciate you being honest," the lead investigator stated, leaning over the scratched metal table. "But why not go to your superiors when you first saw the currency being diverted?"

"Because I'll end up in a lake dead before it's my time," Hammon said bluntly, his voice devoid of any hesitation. "The inner loop doesn't tolerate whistleblowers. You don't get demoted—you vanish."

The investigator checked his notes. "What are you going to do when the prosecutor goes after you for the six hundred thousand you pocketed?"

"I have recordings they don't know about,"Hammon replied, a cold, confident smile touching his lips.

"You do know the USSA have teams of investigators who can get into your phone and computers?" Miller asked, his pen poised.

"I am aware, but I know things they don't know about," Hammon stated smoothly. "Look, I'm pretending to be a dirty cop, and I will get away with anything because of qualified immunity. I know no two cases are alike, so I will never be prosecuted under the current civil rights statutes. My exposure is legally insulated. I just want innocent men and women released from prison."

The lead investigator leaned closer into the glare of the overhead light. "No federal judge will release these people on your word, Hammon. They need proof."

"I have audio and video of how they split the money before it's counted," Hammon revealed, his eyes locking onto the camera lens. "I have the physical tapes of the field splits inside the tracking vans."

"And you are willing to come forward and risk your job to expose this?"

"Yes, I have no choice. I'm in fear for my life."

"Why would you be in fear of your life?" the investigator pushed.

"I've seen horrible things done to people who were thought to be committing crimes," Hammon whispered, his hands tightening inside his cuffs. "I can only imagine what happens to someone who exposes them from the inside. The state machine doesn't protect its own when the money trail is broken."

The investigator flipped the page to the final section of the debriefing protocol. "Were you debriefed by the regional director?"

"Yes."

"What can you tell us about the ticket scheme and overtime logs?"

"I watched agents working second and third jobs while also getting paid by the FBS," Hammon recited flatly. "They were billing the federal task force for hours they spent running private security for local commercial developers."

"And you never reported it?" Miller asked.

"My job was to document corruption," Hammon countered simply. "You can't catch the fish if you pull the net out too early."

The lead investigator tapped the digital recorder. "Agent Hammon, were you asked to attend a deposition regarding the Canal Street raid?"

"Yes."

"Did you?"

"Yes."

"Were you truthful during your deposition?"

"Yes."

"Did you leave out any crime you or others have ever committed?"

Hammon paused, a long, calculating silence filling the concrete room before he met the investigator's gaze. "Yes."

The investigator's posture turned instantly rigid. "What is it?"

"We were able to find money in a lot of these places because of infrared surveillance," Hammon revealed, exposing the hidden baseline of the entire operation.

Miller looked up, astounded. "Did you obtain a warrant for the thermal sweeps?"

"Sometimes," Hammon said, his voice dropping into a chillingly matter-of-fact tone. "Other times, the judge knew they weren't telling the truth."

"Who is 'they'?" the lead investigator demanded.

"My team," Hammon stated flatly.

The investigator leaned completely across the table. "You are able to see the money in homes and businesses using infrared technology?"

"Yes," Hammon said, his expression completely unyielding. "The thermal sensors don't just track body heat, Miller. They map out density differentials behind drywall and flooring. A dense brick of tightly bound paper currency leaves a distinct cold signature relative to the surrounding insulation."

The lead investigator clicked his pen, staring hard at the former agent. "How did you know where the money was?"

"There would be aerial surveillance teams over the suspects' homes," Hammon explained, the spools of the machine capturing the final page of his confession. "And we could see them going in and walking around the house. We watched the heat signatures move to the floorboards, stay stationary for three minutes, and come back up empty-handed. They showed us exactly where they buried the cash, and we just waited until they left the property to go in and take it."

The small, reinforced interrogation cell felt smaller now, the heavy concrete walls seemingly absorbing the weight of Agent Hammon's continuous, chilling admissions. The red recording light on the digital console pulsed steadily, tracking the voice patterns of a man who had spent three years inside corruption school.

The lead investigator leaned forward, his hands flat against the scratched steel table. "You were authorized to fly over suspects' homes and see inside them?"

"No, we didn't have a warrant," Hammon stated smoothly, his voice devoid of any hesitation.

Miller stopped typing, his pen frozen over his notepad. "How many times did this happen?"

"Hundreds of times," Hammon replied. He adjusted his weight in the metal chair, the chains of his handcuffs clinking sharply against the frame. "The flight paths were automated. We treated the whole residential sector of the capital as an open field."

The lead investigator's eyes narrowed into sharp slits under the harsh fluorescent light. "How did you get the money?"

"Oftentimes we waited until they moved it," Hammon explained, a cold, detached expression crossing his face.

"Other times we kicked in the door as a home invasion. If the thermal mapping showed a high-density cache shifting locations late at night, we didn't wait for a federal magistrate to sign off on a raid layout. We went in heavy, masked, and anonymous. The street networks blamed rival factions, and we walked out with the cash splits before the local patrol units even received the dispatch."

The second investigator flipped the folder forward, targeting the roadside weapons sweeps executed by the internet tracking team. "Agent Hammon, did you have a warrant to scan individuals you suspected of carrying firearms?"

"No," Hammon said flatly. "We are to protect the American citizens at any cost, and that is considered an exigent circumstance."

Miller frowned, leaning over the scratched metal partition. "What is an exigent circumstance in the context of an unverified digital sweep?"

"When someone in the public calls law enforcement about a person having a gun, we have to investigate," Hammon stated, his tone dropping into a practiced, bureaucratic cadence. "The safety algorithm overrides the standard procedural boundaries the moment a threat vector is entered into the system."

The lead investigator leaned completely across the table, his posture turning aggressively critical. "So, I can call the police on someone, and you automatically begin scanning their homes and cars for weapons?"

"We can," Hammon admitted without a shred of remorse.

"And it never dawned on you that you were violating the civil rights of these individuals?" the investigator demanded, his voice echoing sharply against the concrete.

Hammon looked directly into the lens of the recording camera, his expression completely unyielding. "I was doing my job."

The lead investigator hit the pause button on the recorder, the tiny spools freezing instantly.

He rubbed his temples, sliding his chair back as he looked over at his partner. Outside the room, the legal team was already assembling the fallout briefs.

"Hammon was right," the investigator muttered, his voice heavy with institutional exhaustion. "They were dirty from top to bottom. Dishonesty is a frequent problem within the interdiction units, but the paperwork cleans it up before it hits the files."

Miller closed his legal pad with a quiet thud. "Qualified immunity—that's all I hear in the briefing rooms. The shield covers everything. But the honest guys on the highway patrols are the ones who suffer. Good cops have to endure the public scrutiny because of a few bad apples."

The legal battle lines shifted dramatically from the back-room interrogations of the capital complex to the wood-paneled, high-ceilinged theater of the Americana Federal Courthouse. The air inside the gallery was thick, charged with the nervous energy of a high-stakes corporate and civil trial.

Bob, the senior defense attorney, stood at the podium facing the packed rows of prospective jurors. His expression was fierce, his posture carved from twenty-five years of street-level litigation.

"The government can seize your home, your business, your car, your cash—regardless of whether or not you've been convicted or even charged with a crime," Bob announced, his voice booming through the courtroom, drawing a sharp glare from the prosecution table.

He leaned against the wooden railing of the jury box, locking eyes with the potential jurors." All my life I've fought. I fight the fucking snitches, I fight the undercover narks, the undercover FBS. When I'm best is when I'm cross-examining a motherfucking snitch. Cross-examination is a trial lawyers weapon. I've been going after snitches for almost 25 years. I will never represent a snitch- never have, never will."

He turned toward the center aisle, gesturing to the heavy binders of discovery material. "The architecture of a federal case is entirely asymmetrical. One side can go out and buy witnesses. If we go out and buy witnesses, we will be prosecuted instantly under federal tampering statutes. But the government can offer freedom, cash, housing, and clean dockets to manufacture the exact testimony they need to secure a percentage on their conviction rates."

He tapped the wooden ledge before the front row of jurors. "Today, jury selection. Can you be fair and impartial when the state presents a ghost asset? Can you spot an incentivized informant? They are the number one cause of wrongful conviction in Union South. Jury selection is an art, and I need to know if you can look past the badge to see the trap."

Miller closed his legal pad with a quiet thud. "Qualified immunity—that's all I hear in the briefing rooms. The shield covers everything. But the honest guys on the highway patrols are the ones who suffer. Good cops have to endure the public scrutiny because of a few bad apples."

conviction in Union South. Jury selection is an art, and I need to know if you can look past the badge to see the trap."

The federal judge took the bench, his gavel hitting the block with a sharp, final echo that silenced the murmurs in the gallery. He adjusted his glasses, looking down over the podium.

"State's first witness," the judge ordered flatly.

Assistant United States Attorney Chambers stood up from the government table, smoothing her dark blazer before stepping to the center podium. She adjusted the microphone, her expression rigid and calculated.

"Please tell the members of the jury your first name," AUSA Chambers directed, turning her head toward the witness box.

The figure sitting on the stand was entirely obscured.

He wore a heavy, non-reflective dark jacket with the collar pinned high, a low-brimmed hat, and dark tactical glasses that completely masked his facial features. The gallery leaned forward, a wave of whispers breaking across the rows.

"Charles," the witness replied, his voice distorted slightly by the heavy fabric covering his jaw.

Chambers stepped closer to the box, wanting to establish the dramatic baseline for the jury immediately. "Charles, why are you on the stand in a disguise?"

The witness shifted uncomfortably, his gloved hands tightening around the edge of the wooden railing. "Because I fear for my life."

Chambers nodded slowly, turning her eyes toward the defense table to measure Bob's reaction. "Where do you currently live?"

The question hung in the heavy silence of the courtroom. Charles shifted his weight, his gloved fingers tightening on the edge of the wood.

"I live at a secure location provided by the federal government," Charles answered, his distorted voice rasping through the audio filter.

Bob didn't wait for AUSA Chambers to ask her next question. He stood up slowly from the defense table, his eyes fixed entirely on the masked figure. The jury watched him, the tension in the room stretching to a thin, dangerous line.

"Your Honor," Bob said, his voice echoing cleanly off the high timber ceilings. "The government has brought a ghost into this room. A ghost who expects us to believe a manufactured script while hiding behind tactical glasses and a fake accent."

Chambers slammed her palm flat against her table. "Objection, Your Honor! The witness has a documented protective status due to threats against his life."

"Overruled," the judge stated icily, gesturing for Bob to proceed. "The defense has a right to explore the parameters of the witness's identity under the Confrontation Clause."

Bob stepped away from his table, walking deliberately toward the center aisle until he was standing directly in front of the jury box. He turned his face toward the twelve citizens sitting in thc rows.

"The government can seize your home, your business, your car, your cash—regardless of whether or not you've been convicted or even charged with a crime," Bob stated, his tone dropping to a gravelly, intense register. "They use ghosts like Charles to clean up the paperwork. They use incentivize files to make you believe an illusion."

He turned back to face the stand, his posture hardening. "All my life I've fought. I fight the fucking snitches, I fight the undercover narks, the undercover FBS. When I'm best is when I'm cross-examining a motherfucking snitch. Cross-examination is a trial lawyer's weapon. I've been going after snitches for almost 25 years. I will never represent a snitch—never have, never will."

Charles pulled his head back slightly into the high collar of his jacket, his shielded eyes tracking Bob's movement.

"One side can go out and buy witnesses," Bob declared, pointing a finger directly at Chambers. "If we go out and buy witnesses, we will be prosecuted instantly. But they can give this man a new life, a tax-free disbursement, and an absolute pass on his own crimes just to get him to point a finger at the defense table."

Bob stepped directly up to the witness box, leaning his forearms against the wooden rail, forcing the masked witness to look down at him.

"Now, Charles—if that is your real name," Bob whispered, his voice cutting sharply through the room. "Let's talk about the hotel room you stayed in for the six weeks leading up to this trial. Let's talk about who paid the bill."

Bob stepped back from the witness stand, his finger pointing directly at the masked figure named Charles. "We never figured it out," Bob said, his voice lowering to a dangerous, steady vibration that filled the entire gallery. "But we did know they weren't using law enforcement data. They were fishing in the dark."

AUSA Chambers stood up, smoothing her blazer, trying to salvage the line of questioning before the jury lost focus. "Did you have a wiretap on this agent?" she asked Charles, leaning onto her podium.

"Yes," Charles rasped through the digital audio filter.

"What did it reveal?"

"The defendant and an unknown male were using an IMSI catcher, listening to phone conversations of members of Congress and other high-profile individuals," Charles revealed.

Bob slammed his fist onto the defense table, his voice booming over the courtroom speakers. "Objection! This is highly prejudicial, uncorrupted, and completely fabricated out of thin air!"

The federal judge didn't let the shouting match expand. He raised his hand, his expression turning ice-cold as he looked toward the twelve citizens sitting in the box. "Members of the jury, you are dismissed for today. We will see you tomorrow morning at nine o'clock flat."

The moment the heavy wooden doors clicked shut behind the jurors, the professional veneer in the room shattered completely.

AUSA Chambers stepped directly to the center podium, her face flushing with anger as she addressed the bench. "Judge, we would like to bring to the court's attention that the defendant is using this same technology that they used in this crime. They are actively manipulating data outside this room."

Bob didn't flinch. He raised a fresh stack of logs he had pulled from his briefcase. "Your Honor, after receiving this information, the defense needs time to question one of the assistant U.S. attorneys. We have data trails pointing directly to the prosecutor's private server. Why would the FBS have to warn good cops to be careful? Because they are recording dirty cops! The entire matrix has turned inward."

By 5:30 PM, the local media vehicles had completely surrounded the courthouse plaza, their satellite dishes tracking the low cloud line where the invisible drones continued their steady, looping flight paths.

"12 News Network breaking news," John's voice cut through the studio monitors as the live feed flashed across the Americana television screens. "Defense attorney loses it in the court. The

structural collapse of the federal case against local businessmen has turned into an open war between the legal defense bar and the Department of Justice."

The camera cut to Bob walking down the stone steps of the courthouse, completely surrounded by reporters.

"This is a dirty prosecutor!" Bob shouted into the cluster of microphones, his eyes burning with intense conviction. "There are innocent men and women sitting in prison because of the games played inside that building! They aren't getting a wiretap order, ladies and gentlemen. They are turning the mic on your phone! If you have the phone anywhere near you while having a conversation, they can just turn on the mic and listen, or turn on the camera and record it."

Behind the camera crew, the network technicians were checking their own mobile devices, watching their signal bars fluctuate erratically as an unmarked surveillance van rolled past the curb.

"This prosecutor is dirty," John stated cleanly into his microphone, taking over the broadcast narration. "The tracking parameters are absolute. Our sources inside the complex have confirmed the directive: have your people cover up their phone cameras, and not to have personal conversations near your phone."

Inside the news van, the chief audio editor looked at his laptop screen. "What if I turn the phone off?"

"It doesn't matter," John's voiceover continued over the live B-roll footage of the capital towers. "It really isn't off. You would have to take the battery completely out of the phone to kill the tracking chip. This is beyond the FBS. Someone at the Office of the Inspector General needs to open an investigation into these corrupt prosecutors."

The systemic rot was no longer a secret contained within the archive folders. Corrupt prosecutors are in cahoots with dirty cops and federal agents who go out and frame innocent civilians. Entrapment cases are never taken to trial because most defendants don't go to trial; they take the plea deal out of raw terror, so they never get a chance to question their accuser. The sixth amendment had been entirely replaced by a data entry loop.

Corrupt federal agents are going out recruiting informants to entrap defendants who they think may commit crimes, engineering the very violations they are paid to discover.

Inside the defense war room, Bob reviewed the electronic logs with his trial team. "My client has recorded every day of his life for years in order to prove how cops get on the stand and lie, frame, abuse, and murder innocent people. He turned his whole environment into a black box recorder. We are putting together a mock jury to test the reaction to the original analog tapes. I know for a fact many men have been convicted on an informant's testimony alone, but when the jury sees the physical setup, the consensus shifts."

The lead investigator tapped a line on the local police budget report. "Why can't the police talk about lowering hiring standards? Will they ever talk about the ticket scheme or overtime theft?"

"No," Bob said flatly. "A dirty cop can get caught red-handed, and the police union will move the goalpost to protect the pension structure. The accountability is entirely cosmetic."

On Monday morning, the courtroom was packed to maximum capacity. The air was dead silent as Agent Hammon was called back to the stand under a strict defense subpoena. Bob stepped to the podium, his posture rigid.

"Agent Hammon, why are you coming forward now?" Bob demanded.

"Because it's the right thing to do," Hammon answered, his voice echoing clearly against the high timber walls.

"Did you contribute to this?"

"Yes," Hammon admitted, looking toward the jury box. "That's why I want to make it right."

Bob leaned against the wooden rail, his expression turning sharp. "So, why did you instruct the crime lab to falsify drug tests?"

Hammon blinked, his hands tightening on the armrests. "I don't know what you mean."

"You asked a member of the crime lab to say sheetrock was cocaine, when you knew it was not," Bob declared, pulling a certified laboratory email string from his binder.

AUSA Chambers jumped to her feet, her chair scraping loudly across the linoleum. "Your Honor, the state would like a sidebar!"

The judge didn't hesitate, slamming his gavel down twice. "Members of the jury are excused until Monday morning. Clear the room."

Once the gallery was emptied, Chambers leaned across the judge's bench, her voice tight with panic. "Your Honor, the state would like to present state secrets because of what the defense has uncovered. The tracking infrastructure and the laboratory protocols are protected under national security mandates."

"The people of Union South want to know the government is being transparent and not framing innocent citizens," Bob countered fiercely, stepping up to the bench. "What we are looking at here, Your Honor, is *testilying*. It's an institutional practice. When did this agent lie? Did he lie on the 602? Did he lie to the grand jury? Or is he lying in court, Your Honor? You can't make this up! Even if you gave this script to Hollywood, they wouldn't believe it."

Bob turned, facing the empty gallery before looking back at the bench. "Your Honor, we would like the court to dismiss all charges against my clients. The government intentionally set out to frame innocent civilians using informants who were proven guilty of lying in the past."

The judge stared down at the documents, his face a mask of bureaucratic stone. He didn't rule on the motion, shifting his eyes toward the witness list.

"Your Honor, we call our next witness," Bob announced, refusing to let the momentum break.

A local field informant, stripped of his asset protection numbers, stepped into the box. Bob didn't waste time with preliminaries.

"Have you ever tried to contact my client?" Bob asked sharply.

"No, sir," the witness replied, staring down at his lap.

"No?" Bob questioned, his voice dripping with sarcasm. "Your Honor, can we play a video for the witness?"

The judge nodded. "You may."

The screen in the center of the courtroom flared to life, showing an unedited hidden-camera feed from a commercial parking lot. Bob pointed to the figure on the display. "This is you, correct?"

"Yes," the witness whispered.

"What are you doing?"

"Trying to contact your client."

CHAPTER EIGHT

Bob stepped directly up to the box, his voice crashing through the room." But you just told this court you had not!"

The witness cracked, his hands shaking as he looked toward the prosecution table. "The prosecutor told me to lie! They sat me in the back room and said, *'We need you to say you witnessed everything that is written on that paper.'* I told them I don't want to lie to the judge, but the handler said, *'I need you to say everything on that paper, or you're going to prison.'"*

The courtroom went completely dead silent. Bob looked at Chambers, then at the judge, exposing the absolute fault line of the entire judicial system.

"Some of these are serious crimes," Bob murmured, his voice cold and steady as he looked at the redacted folders. "And this prosecutor has dropped these cases down to misdemeanors because they are members of law enforcement or assets of the task force. Why can't the members of poor communities be awarded this same standard of leniency?"

Bob's voice cracked through the microphoned speakers of the courtroom like a gunshot, his hand slamming into the oak wood paneling of the podium. He did not look at the jury; he kept his eyes locked straight on AUSA Chambers.

"This is a travesty of justice!" Bob roared, the veins in his neck tightening into thick cords. "Fourth Amendment rights are being violated, and these agents are being promoted for sending innocent people to prison. The record shows the initial Title Three wiretap was denied. Denied by a federal magistrate! Yet they ran the frequency anyway, and now they expect this court to bless the fruits of a poisoned extraction."

He turned sharply, addressing the bench.

"Your Honor, we ask that the Justice Department come in and investigate the entire DEA. Not only was this defendant charged with conspiracy to sell narcotics, he was charged with felony

arson. Your Honor, my client was charged with putting his co-defendants home on fire." But look at the database trail we've forced into the light! This same co-defendant is a federal informant, and has been since the late 80's, while selling cocaine under the eye of the DEA!"

Bob stepped into the center aisle, his arms raised to encompass the entire gallery.

"We have uncovered agents involved in robbing drug dealers, moving about the country framing innocent individuals, and pressuring witnesses to lie. We ask for a mistrial."

The judge didn't blink. He raised his gavel, dropping it once with a hollow, unyielding thud. "Motion denied."

Bob let out a short, furious breath, turning back to his table. "All we hear is state secrets. They bring my client into court, and we prove these are corrupt prosecutors. Like cowards, they claim state secrets. They are flying planes stealing data from American citizens, violating their civil rights, kidnapping journalists, and then telling us we are free."

The line on John's encrypted newsroom monitor split, a fresh wave of data pouring across the digital partition from his source inside the security compound. John gripped the receiver tightly against his ear.

"Wait, what?" John whispered, his eyes scanning the new text coordinates. "Kidnapping journalists?"

"Yes," the gravelly voice crackled over the secure channel. "Journalists are disappearing, John. From what I'm told, they are being waterboarded and tortured like terrorists for exposing corruption."

John felt the cold sweat return to his collar. "How do you know these things?"

"I can't tell you," the contact replied instantly. "If we bring light to it, maybe they won't do it anymore."

"Look, John," the voice continued, dropping into a chillingly flat register. "These are government assassins. They could care less what is reported on the news."

John's pen paused over his notepad. "You're telling me the government has hired hitmen to kill anyone that can expose corruption?"

"That's what I'm telling you."

John closed his eyes, the absolute scale of the invisible infrastructure pressing down on him. "I'm not asking you to tell me anymore. Just point me in the direction I need to look."

"Federal prosecutions in the last twenty years," the contact directed smoothly. "Grand juries in drug cases, and the jury process."

"Anything else?"

"Search libraries. I wouldn't go to the court or search anything on the internet."

John frowned. "Why?"

"They can track you," the contact warned before the line went completely dead. "And figure out very quickly what you're doing."

The recess ended, and the court roared back to life. Bob stood at the defense podium, his expression entirely carved from stone as he checked the next name on his subpoena list.

"Your Honor, the defense would like to bring in Agent Nowatzski's wife," Bob announced.

AUSA Chambers jumped to her feet instantly. "Objection, Your Honor! The defense is trying to discredit this agent. The personal domestic history of an operative has zero relevance to the active evidentiary layout."

"Your Honor," Bob countered fiercely, turning to face the jury box. "The defense wants to show the members of the jury that this agent is not truthful to his wife, so how can the jury believe him under oath?"

The judge adjusted his glasses, looking between the two tables before hitting his gavel. "I'll allow it."

The heavy wooden doors opened, and a quiet woman in a plain dark blouse walked down the center aisle, taking her seat inside the witness box.

"State your name for the members of the jury," the clerk directed.

"Ann Nowatzski," she said, her voice thin.

Bob stepped forward, keeping his distance respectful but firm. "Mrs. Nowatzski, what do you do for a living?"

"I'm a homemaker."

"Has your husband ever told you he cheated on you?"

"No," she whispered, looking down at her hands.

Bob turned back to his table, pulling a digital playback module from his case. "Your Honor, the defense would like to play back the testimony from Agent Nowatzski."

Chambers slammed her folder down. "Objection! Side bar, Your Honor!"

The judge sighed, waving them toward the bench while gesturing to the bailiff. "Members of the jury, we will take a small recess for lunch."

Inside the closed chambers, Chambers turned on Bob, her face red. "Your Honor, the personal life of an agent has nothing to do with his professional life."

"That is true," the judge noted coldly, looking down at the prosecutor. "But this is your witness, and the defense should be able to check the credibility of this witness. If he lies beneath his own roof, the jury has a right to weigh his oath."

When the court reconvened, Bob faced the homemaker once more. "Mrs. Nowatzski, you were able to see the video of your husband's testimony?"

"Yes."

"Did you know your husband was having affairs?"

"I did not know," she said clearly.

Bob nodded, stepping back. "That's it for this witness. We recall Agent Nowatzski."

The veteran field agent stepped back into the box, his expression rigid and defensive. Bob didn't let him settle.

"Agent Nowatzski, were you involved in a payroll fraud scheme?"

"No," the agent snapped.

"Were you ever questioned about a payroll scheme?"

Nowatzski hesitated, his eyes shifting toward Chambers. "Yes."

"Can you tell the members of the jury about the investigation?"

"I wasn wasn't involved, so I don't know," the agent parried.

Bob pulled a redacted internal affairs sheet from his binder. "You were accused of helping those convicted of overtime theft, but there wasn't enough evidence to convict you."

"I have no idea what happened during that case," Nowatzski stated flatly.

"Pass the witness," Bob said.

Chambers stood up, trying to rebuild the line. "Agent Nowatzski, did the FBS do a financial workup on you?"

"Yes."

"Were you told by the FBS that you owe them money, because your lifestyle exceeded your income?"

"Yes," the agent admitted under the pressure of the audit records.

Chambers crossed her arms. "Why would you agree to something you didn't do?"

Nowatzski let out a tired, cynical sigh. "It was cheaper to negotiate a plea than fight it."

"Next witness," the clerk called.

A man wearing a crisp, commercial pilot's uniform stepped into the courtroom, his gold bars catching the overhead lights as he took the oath.

"State your name for the jury."

"James McDonald."

Bob stepped to the podium. "Mr. McDonald, what do you do for a living?"

"I'm a pilot for the Union South government," McDonald answered proudly.

"Are you part of an elite surveillance team?"

"Yes."

"What do you do?"

"We follow suspected criminals," the pilot explained calmly.

"Have you ever followed someone who wasn't committing crimes?" Bob asked, his voice dropping into a sharp focus.

"Yes, plenty of times," McDonald admitted without thinking.

"Do you know of any federal agents who have set up suspects?"

"Never," the pilot stated firmly.

"When the defense says agents are framing suspects, what would you say?" Bob pressed, stepping closer to the box.

McDonald looked directly at the jury box. "There is no way an agent would risk their career or freedom."

Bob smiled, a cold, predatory expression. "I pass this witness."

Chambers didn't stand, but Bob remained in the center aisle, turning back toward the pilot before he could step down. "Mr. McDonald, have you ever used cocaine?"

McDonald's face tightened instantly. "What do you mean?"

"It's a yes or no question," Bob barked, his voice echoing off the high walls. "Have you ever used cocaine?"

"No," the pilot said, his jaw rigid.

"Defense would like to play evidence 360," Bob announced, gesturing toward his tech desk.

The judge checked the evidence ledger. "Defense evidence 360 can be published."

The primary projector screen dropped from the ceiling, flaring to life with a high-definition video captured inside a smoky local tavern. On the screen, McDonald was clearly visible, laughing

with a group of men as he leaned over a glass table, using a rolled bill to draw a white line into his nose.

Bob hit the pause button, leaving the pilot's face frozen on the screen in absolute clarity. "Mr. McDonald, what are you doing here?"

McDonald swallowed hard, his face flushing crimson under his collar. "Playing around with friends at the bar."

"So, you are pretending to be snorting cocaine?" Bob asked, his tone dripping with sarcasm.

"Yes."

"Are these friends you're playing around with going to corroborate your story?"

"Yes," McDonald whispered.

Bob clicked the monitor off. "Nothing further from this witness."

The judge looked at the clock, his expression completely exhausted as he raised his gavel. "Recess till Monday."

Inside the defense war room later that evening, the team collapsed into their leather chairs, surrounded by empty coffee cups and open files.

"Today was brutal," the investigator muttered, rubbing his eyes.

John looked up from his laptop, a grim smile on his face. "Wait until Monday. They will never see it coming."

The investigator tilted his head. "What's going on?"

"An inmate who has been in solitary for years has been put in general population," John revealed, showing an internal transit log from the maximum-security wing.

"What does that have to do with us?"

"He was beaten, starved, and hidden for disciplinary reasons so he couldn't testify," John explained, his voice rising with intense focus. "They locked him away to keep his deposition out of our dockets. Tonight on 12 News Investigates: *Even judges hate jailhouse snitches.*"

The blue light of the television monitors cut through the darkness of the office as the pre-recorded segment hit the air. On the screen, a leaked transcript from a judicial review panel displayed a sharp confrontation between a district magistrate and the prosecution team.

"Did you put on a jailhouse snitch and didn't investigate it?" the judge's text read on the screen.

"More from the trial of the century at nine," John's broadcast narration announced to the city. "This Union South attorney is a piece of work. You knowingly took cases from dirty federal agents and didn't tell the defense. The people of this country should be told the truth."

Outside the studio, a reporter cornered the acting prosecutor near his vehicle. "Are they investigating the acting Union South attorney?"

The official refused to look at the camera, his hands shaking as he unlocked his car door. "I can't confirm or deny anything at this point."

"They are investigating him," John's voiceover concluded as the screen cut back to the studio. "Once this is over, the court is going to be backed up for years because of corruption."

On Monday morning, the atmosphere inside the courthouse was electric. Before the jury could even enter the room, Bob stood at

the center podium, his hand resting on a fresh stack of internal memos he had secured over the weekend.

"Your Honor," Bob announced, his voice tight. "AUSA Chambers showed discovery to one of his witnesses and prepared her for our questioning. He coached the asset using the very files we fought to unredact. This is a corrupt prosecutor, and he should be removed."

Chambers stood up, his face tight. "This is ridiculous, Judge!"

"We have information that this AUSA instructed federal agents to threaten members of my client's family," Bob shouted over the interruption, turning directly to the bench. "We have audio and video of an agent asking DEA agents to frame my client, whom they've known for years. They worked side by side arresting bad guys, and they turned on my client, who is a decorated DEA agent!"

He pointed a finger toward the gallery, where the administrative representatives sat in silence. "Your Honor, these are federal agents with questionable backgrounds, and the Department of Justice should look into them. This agent has been committing crimes for years, and the government has hid his personnel file from the public."

The judge slammed his gavel down three times, the echoes silencing the room. "That's enough. Back in court. Bring in the jurors."

The heavy wooden doors opened, and the twelve citizens filed back into their box, their expressions tense. The judge adjusted his robe, looking down over the podium.

"Members of the jury, the state will give closing arguments," the judge announced.

Bob stood straight at his table, his voice cutting through the room before Chambers could even reach the podium. "Judge, we would like to dismiss all charges before the state starts closing."

The judge didn't look up from his desk, his voice completely flat. "Request denied."

Bob sat back down, his eyes narrowing as he looked toward the recording light of the media box. The machinery of the state was moving toward its final

conclusion, completely indifferent to the exposure. Hammon was right from the very first page inside corruption school—they were dirty, and the dishonesty was just a routine line item in the budget.

The courtroom sat in a heavy, suffocating silence. AUSA Chambers stood at the central podium, her final words to the jury lingering in the humid air like smoke. She didn't talk about the forensic signal logs or the original analog tapes. She talked about the thin blue line. She spoke of structure, of a world that would tear itself apart from the inside if the citizens stopped trusting the gold badges of the task force.

Bob didn't look at her as she sat down. He sat with his hands clasped flat against the mahogany table, his eyes locked onto the closed door of the jury deliberation room.

Four hours passed before the heavy brass handle clicked.

The gallery leaned forward in unison, the fabric of dozens of suits rustling against the oak benches. The twelve citizens filed back into their box, their expressions completely unreadable under the dim, historic chandelier light.

"Have you reached a verdict?" the judge asked, his voice entirely flat.

"We have, Your Honor," the foreperson stated, standing straight.

Bob felt his chest tighten as the clerk took the slip of paper, stepping up to the bench. The judge scanned the lines with a mask of bureaucratic stone, his face revealing absolutely nothing before he handed the document back down.

"On the count of conspiracy to distribute controlled substances," the clerk read, the words echoing off the high timber ceilings. "We find the defendant... guilty."

A sharp, collective intake of breath cut through the defense side of the gallery. Bob didn't move. He didn't slam his hand down. A cold, heavy understanding settled into his bones as the clerk ran through the remaining counts—each one falling like a iron gate closing shut. Guilty. Guilty. Guilty.

The judge hit his gavel once, the thud signaling the immediate transition from a trial into an administrative erasure. "Court is adjourned. Sentencing will be scheduled for the fall term."

Chambers began packing her leather trial bags, her face relaxed, her victory completely quiet. She didn't smile; she simply checked the boxes on her docket sheet. The system had held. The exposure, the videotaped frame-ups, the confessions of corruption school—none of it mattered once the jury was reminded of their own fear. They chose the protection of the state over the reality of the wire.

The transition from the wood-paneled courthouse to the maximum-security holding facility at Americana Central happened within thirty minutes. Stripped of his civilian suit and his gold watch, Hammon sat on the edge of a thin, steel bunk, his back pressed against the cold, unpainted concrete wall of his cell.

The noise of the trial had completely vanished, replaced by the low, mechanical drone of the facility's centralized air system. Through the narrow, reinforced window of his cell door, he could see the gray corridor stretching into the darkness.

"Should I have taken the stand?" Hammon whispered to the empty room, his voice raspy and thin. "Who could I have trusted?"

He let out a short, hollow laugh, looking down at his orange jumpsuit. The questions had circled his mind for three years, a looping track of self-examination that always ended at the same wall. He had spent his entire career learning how to manipulate targets, how to turn an innocent narrative into a multi-million-dollar felony, and in the end, the machine had simply run the exact same protocol on him.

The heavy outer gate of the cell block buzzed sharply, the sound of boots echoing against the concrete floors as a guard approached his cell. The slot on the door slid open with a violent metallic crack.

A plain paper tray was pushed through the opening, the food inside smelling faintly of industrial cleaner and damp cardboard. Hammon didn't touch it. He remembered the warning from the tracking van: *They will try to feed you spoiled and rotten food. They will put glass, feces, and rat poison in your tray to break your health.*

He leaned his head back against the concrete, closing his eyes. Outside the walls of the complex, the sky over the city was already turning black. Hundreds of autonomous drones were launching from the hidden corporate airstrips, their infrared lenses spinning as they mapped out the heat signatures of unsuspecting citizens walking the blocks below.

The IMSI catchers were cycling through the frequencies, harvesting metadata from cell phones that were supposedly turned off.

At his desk at 12 News Network, John stared at a blinking cursor on a blank screen. His phone had been silent for twelve hours, his sources vanishing back into the shadows the moment the guilty verdict hit the wires. He reached into his drawer, pulling out a small square of black tape, and carefully pressed it over the lens of his webcam. He knew it didn't stop the microphone from streaming, but it was the only boundary he had left.

Deep inside the solitary cells, the noise of the world faded entirely, replaced by the stark clarity of the cage. Doing the right thing in Union South didn't lead to a press conference or a public clearing of the record. It led here. It led to the silence of an administrative block where the paperwork was clean, the dockets were closed, and the state secrets remained buried beneath the concrete.

Hammon turned his face away from the door, his eyes tracking a single line of text he had scratched into the gray paint near his bunk with the edge of a plastic spoon:

The cover-up is worse than the crime, but the wire lasts forever.

DESTRY JARRETT
TO
PILLAR
LIES, THEFT, AND BLOOD:
INSIDE THE MIND OF A COP KILLER
DESTRY JARRETT

EVERYTHING THE WAR ON DRUGS HAS
ACCOMPLISHED IN 55 YEARS
NOTHING
DESTRY JARRETT

TRIAL BY
AMBUSH
FEDERAL AGENT TURNED RAT

FROM KILLER TO PILLAR

Made in the USA
Monee, IL
04 November 2026

67378027R00085